LERNPLUS+

DIE LERNHILFE FÜRS GYMNASIUM

ENGLISCH
5. SCHULJAHR

Schroedel

LERNPLUS+
Englisch 5. Schuljahr

Autoren:
Bernd Raczkowsky
Christof Wagner

ISBN 978-3-507-**23161**-0

Druck 1 / Jahr 2009

Redaktion: Ute Schröder, Katrin Spiller
Herstellung: Dirk von Lüderitz
Umschlaggestaltung und Layout: Janssen Kahlert Design & Kommunikation GmbH, Hannover
Illustrationen: Sarah Burrini, Köln und Matthias Berghahn, Bielefeld
Satz: imprint, Zusmarshausen
Druck und Bindung: westermann druck GmbH, Braunschweig

Liebe Schülerin, lieber Schüler,

Lernplus hilft dir, die wichtigsten Inhalte des Englischunterrichts in der Klasse 5 zu wiederholen, zu üben und besonders die Themen zu trainieren, die erfahrungsgemäß viele Stolpersteine enthalten. Mit Lernplus kannst du deine Wissenslücken schließen, deine Grammatikkenntnisse verbessern und den Umgang mit Texten üben.
Alle Kapitel sind überschaubar gegliedert und alle Regeln werden Schritt für Schritt erklärt, bevor du sie in den Übungen selbstständig anwendest.

Training plus fragt dein Wissen am Ende eines Kapitels noch einmal ab. Mithilfe der insgesamt 99 Testfragen kannst du gut überprüfen, wie sicher du die einzelnen Regeln beherrschst.

Den **Abschlusstest** nach jedem Kapitel bearbeitest du so wie eine Klassenarbeit. In der Regel gibt es für jede Teilaufgabe einen Punkt, bei Übersetzungsaufgaben oder schwierigeren Aufgaben zwei Punkte. In den Lösungen findest du eine Punkteübersicht, mit der du deine Leistungen einschätzen kannst.

In Lernplus gibt es außerdem drei besondere Elemente:

Regel Die Regeln werden in jedem Kapitel verständlich zusammengefasst und anschaulich erklärt. Oft werden sie durch Beispiele ergänzt.

Tipp Hinweise, worauf du beim Lernen achten solltest oder wie du dir etwas besonders gut merken kannst, findest du bei den Tipps.

Info plus Weißt du, was sich hinter dem *Boxing Day* verbirgt oder woher der Dudelsack *(bagpipe)* stammt? Für alle, die etwas mehr wissen wollen, bietet Info plus spannende Informationen oder Hintergründe zu Redewendungen und Vokabeln.

Mithilfe der **Lösungen** im Anhang kannst du kontrollieren, ob du die Aufgaben richtig bearbeitet hast und wie viele Punkte du im Abschlusstest erzielt hast. Wenn du im Buch nicht genügend Platz für die Bearbeitung der Übungen findest, schreibe die Lösungen bitte in ein Heft.

Viel Erfolg beim Üben und Besserwerden mit Lernplus wünscht dir

das **Lernplus-Team**

1 Grundlegende Satzbausteine

Wer mit der englischen Sprache richtig umgehen will, muss ihre Grundbausteine kennen. Mit diesen Bausteinen lassen sich – richtig zusammengesetzt – einfache, sinnvolle Sätze bilden. Fülle deinen sprachlichen „Werkzeugkasten" also mit geeigneten Werkzeugen und Materialien auf.

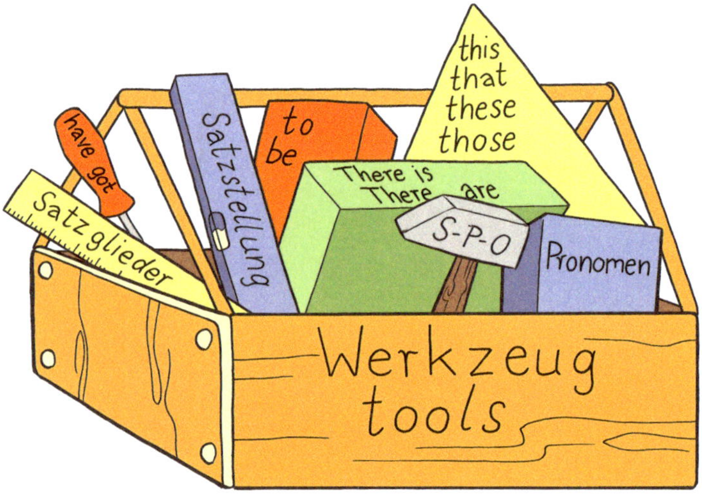

1.1 Satz und Satzglieder

Regel

Satzglieder

Die Satzglieder **Subjekt**, **Prädikat** und **Objekt** gibt es nicht nur im Deutschen, sondern auch im Englischen. Hier heißen sie ***subject***, ***predicate*** und ***object***. Diese drei Satzteile kannst du im Deutschen und im Englischen sehr schnell bestimmen:

Ich lese Bücher. → *Ich* = Subjekt; *lese* = Prädikat; *Bücher* = Objekt
I read books. → *I = subject; read = predicate; books = object*

So fragst du nach Subjekt, Prädikat und Objekt:

Subjekt	**Prädikat**	**Objekt**
Wer oder Was?	Was tut das Subjekt? Was wird getan?	Wen oder Was?
Ich	*lese*	*Bücher.*
I	*read*	*books.*

1 Unterstreiche in jedem deutschen und englischen Satz das Subjekt *(subject)* blau, das Prädikat *(predicate)* rot und das Objekt *(object)* grün.

a) Meine Eltern lesen Zeitungen.

My parents read newspapers.

b) Können wir diese Geschichte erzählen?

Can we tell this story?

c) Du liebst italienisches Essen.

You love Italian food.

d) Die Katze meines Freundes frisst Mäuse.

My friend's cat eats mice.

2 Bilde einfache englische Aussagesätze. Nutze dabei die drei Körbe.

a) Dr. Sixt ______

b) She ______

c) Beyoncé ______

d) My dog ______

e) Mike ______

f) Sarah ______

g) Peter ______

1.2 Personalpronomen (Subjektfall) und die Formen von *to be*

Regel

Die Personalpronomen im Subjektfall

- Die folgende Tabelle zeigt die **Personalpronomen** bzw. Fürwörter *(personal pronouns)* im Subjektfall *(subject case)*.

	Singular	Plural
1. Person	**I** - ich	**we** - wir
2. Person	**you** - du	**you** - ihr
3. Person	**he, she, it** - er, sie, es	**they** - sie

- Im Englischen wird ***I* immer großgeschrieben**, egal ob es am Satzanfang oder an irgendeiner anderen Stelle im Satz steht!

Regel

Die Formen von *to be* (sein)

Langform:	I **am**	you **are**	he **is**	she **is**	it **is**	we **are**	you **are**	they **are**
Kurzform:	I**'m**	you**'re**	he**'s**	she**'s**	it**'s**	we**'re**	you**'re**	they**'re**

3 Übersetze jeden Satz nach folgendem Muster:

Personalpronomen + Form von *be* + Adjektiv

a) Ich bin nervös *(nervous)*. ______________________.

b) Du bist alt *(old)*. ______________________.

c) Er ist schnell *(fast)*. ______________________.

d) Sie ist aufgeregt *(excited)*. ______________________.

e) Es ist regnerisch *(rainy)*. ______________________.

f) Wir sind glücklich *(happy)*. ______________________.

g) Ihr seid traurig *(sad)*. ______________________.

h) Sie sind müde *(tired)*. ______________________.

1.3 Die Verneinung von *to be*

Regel

Verneinung von *be*

Die Verneinungen von *be* in den verschiedenen Personen lauten:

Person	**Normalform**	**Kurzform**
1. Person, **Singular**	I am not	I'm not
2. Person, **Singular**	you are not	you aren't / you're not
3. Person, **Singular**	he is not she is not it is not	he isn't / he's not she isn't / she's not it isn't / it's not
1. Person, **Plural**	we are not	we aren't / we're not
2. Person, **Plural**	you are not	you aren't / you're not
3. Person, **Plural**	they are not	they aren't / they're not

4 Verneine jeden Aussagesatz mit den beiden Kurzformen.

a) Peter is twelve. → Peter isn't twelve. He's not twelve.

b) We are strong. → ______

c) You are a boy. → ______

d) I am a girl. → ______

e) Susan is late. → ______

f) Tom and Paul are here. → ______

g) It is cold. → ______

h) You are tired. → ______

i) She is Irish. → ______

j) It is too late. → ______

k) They are angry → ______

l) I am hungry. → ______

5 Bilde Sätze nach folgendem Muster. Verwende jeweils die Kurzform.

a) *Sarah isn't happy, she's sad.*

a) Sarah

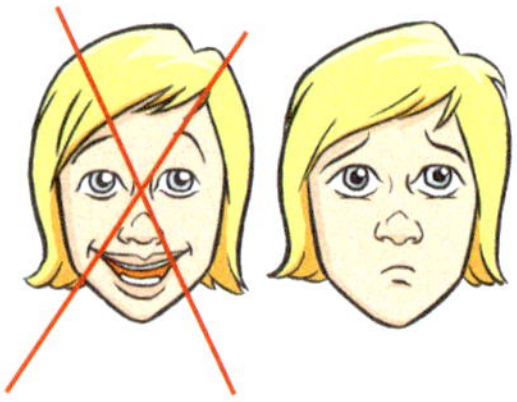

happy sad

b) The house

big small

c) Mr and Mrs Miller

here over there

d) Peter

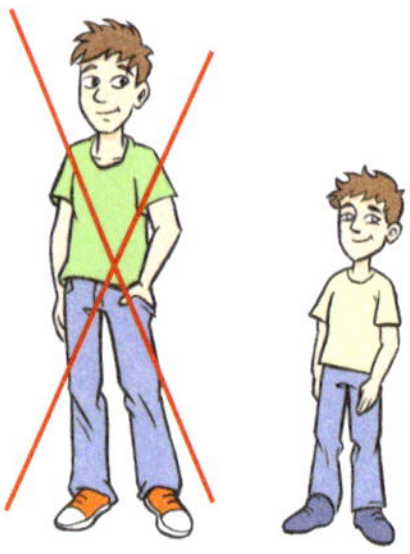

tall short

e) You

f) The girl

to be good at

____

____

____

____

____

____

____

____

____

1.4 Fragen mit *be* und Kurzantworten

Regel

Fragen mit *be*

Bei einfachen Fragen mit *be* werden **Personalpronomen** und die **Form von *be*** einfach **vertauscht**.

Aussagesatz		**Fragesatz**
He is thirteen.	→	*Is he thirteen?*
We are tourists.	→	*Are we tourists?*

6 Vervollständige die Tabelle.

deutsch (Aussagesatz)	**englisch (Frage, bejaht)**	**englisch (Frage, verneint)**	**englisch (Frage, verneint, Kurzform)**
Du bist klug *(clever)*.	Are you clever?	Are you not clever?	Aren't you clever?
	Is Mary funny?		
			Isn't my father a teacher?
		Are the boys not late?	
Er ist aufgeregt *(excited)*.			

Tipp

Wann verwendet man Kurzformen?

In der Regel verwendet man Kurzformen wie *isn't* und *aren't* immer dann, wenn man mit jemandem spricht. Im geschriebenen Englisch werden meist die Normalformen gebraucht, es sei denn, es liegt ein Text in der direkten Rede vor.

Regel

Kurzantworten mit *be*

Auf Fragen mit *be* werden meist Kurzantworten gegeben.
Die Tabelle zeigt diese Kurzantworten.

Am I old?	*Yes, I am.*	*No, I'm not.*
Are you funny?	*Yes, you are.*	*No, you aren't.*
Is he twelve?	*Yes, he is.*	*No, he isn't.*
Is the girl your sister?	*Yes, she is.*	*No, she isn't.*
Is your house big?	*Yes, it is.*	*No, it isn't.*
Are we German?	*Yes, we are.*	*No, we aren't.*
Are you students?	*Yes, you are.*	*No, you aren't*
Are Mr and Mrs Franklin young?	*Yes, they are.*	*No, they aren't.*

7 Setze die entsprechende Kurzantwort ein.

a) Mum: "Pete, are you in your room?" Pete: "No, Mum, ________________."

b) Dad: "Are Susan and Mary at school?" Mum: "No, ________________."

c) Grandpa: "Is Maxwell good at Maths?" Grandma: "Yes, ________________."

d) Tim: "Are we at the concert tonight?" Sue: "Oh yes, ________________."

e) Bill: "It's late. Are you tired?" Ben: "No, ________________."

f) Teacher: "Is Grace ill today?" Pupil: "No, ________________, she's just late."

8 Finde zu jeder Kurzantwort eine passende Frage.

a) ________________________? – No, she isn't. She's nine.

b) ________________________? – Yes, they are.

c) ________________________? – No, we aren't. We are English.

d) ________________________? – Yes, I am.

e) ______________________________ ? – No, it isn't. It's Tuesday.

f) ______________________________ ? – No, he isn't. He's from Leeds.

1.5 Possessivpronomen: *Possessive pronouns*

Regel

Possessivpronomen

Das Possessivpronomen zeigt an, **zu wem etwas gehört** oder wem etwas zuzuordnen ist. Die Possessivpronomen lauten im Englischen wie folgt:

	Singular	**Plural**
1. Person	**my** – mein, meine	**our** – unser, unsere
2. Person	**your** – dein, deine	**your** – euer, euere
3. Person	**his** – sein, seine **her** – ihr, ihre **its** – sein, seine	**their** – ihr, ihre

9 Übersetze und füge das passende Possessivpronomen ein.

dein Lineal ______________	seine Eltern ______________
euer Haus ______________	mein Leben ______________
ihre Kinder (der Leute) ______________	ihre Schwester (zwei Lösungen) ______________
unsere Schule ______________	ihr Bruder (zwei Lösungen) ______________
eure Frage ______________	meine Antwort ______________

1.6 Der *s*-Genitiv

Regel

Der *s*-Genitiv

- Der **s-Genitiv** zeigt an, dass einer Person oder mehreren Personen etwas gehört oder zugeordnet wird. Achtung: Im Englischen steht immer der s-Genitiv, auch wenn im Deutschen die Konstruktion „… von meinem/meiner …" verwendet werden kann!
- Im Singular wird der *s*-Genitiv folgendermaßen gebildet:
  Singularwort + **Apostroph** + ***s***
  Peter's *car – Peters Auto/das Auto von Peter*
  My ***father's*** *house – das Haus meines Vaters*
- Im Plural geht man so vor: Zuerst wird das Bezugswort (Personen) durch ein angehängtes *s* in den Plural gesetzt. Anschließend fügt man – etwas abgesetzt – ein Apostroph hinzu: **Pluralwort** + **Apostroph**
  her ***parents'*** *livingroom – das Wohnzimmer ihrer Eltern*
  our ***neighbours'*** *cat – die Katze unserer Nachbarn*
- Bei ***child***/***children*** liegt ein Sonderfall vor:
  Singular: *Our* ***child's*** *bike …*, aber: *Our* ***children's*** *bikes …*

10 Bilde den *s*-Genitiv.

a) Lea

b) Mr and Mrs Hall

c) His uncle

d) The Millers

e) Frank

f) Her child

g) Her brother

h) Their children

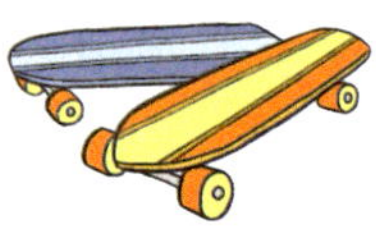

i) Our teacher

a) ____________ b) ____________

c) ____________ d) ____________

e) ____________ f) ____________

g) ____________ h) ____________

i) ____________

11 Übersetze. Schreibe in dein Heft.

Das ist das Haus meiner Tante, Mrs Dexter. Das Fahrrad ihres Sohnes steht vor der Garage mit dem Auto ihres Mannes *(husband)*. Der Hund ihrer Tochter schläft immer im Garten. Das Zuhause *(home)* dieser Familie liegt in der Oak Road. Meine Tante arbeitet außerhalb der Stadt. Sie arbeitet im Krankenhause. Die Kinder meiner Tante kennen dieses Krankenhaus sehr gut.

1.7 Der *of*-Genitiv

Regel

Der *of*-Genitiv

Er wird immer dann verwendet, wenn das **Bezugswort keine Person** ist.

*The walls **of** my room…*	*Die Wände meines Zimmers …*	(Bezugswort: *room*)
*The roof **of** the house …*	*Das Dach des Hauses …*	(Bezugswort: *house*)
*The colour **of** our shirts …*	*Die Farbe unserer Hemden …*	(Bezugswort: *shirts*)

12 Susan war eine Woche in London. Sie berichtet, was sie gesehen und beeindruckt hat. Übersetze.

a) Der Bürgermeister *(mayor)* der Stadt … ____________

b) Der Markt von Camden Town … ____________

c) Die Farbe des Busses … ____________

d) Die Fenster von Westminster Abbey … ____________

e) Das Alter *(age)* der Kronjuwelen *(Crown Jewels)* … ____________

f) Die Länge *(length)* der Tower Bridge … ____________

g) Die Tiefe *(depth)* der Themse *(the river Thames)* … ____________

h) Die Größe *(size)* des Hyde Parks … ____________

i) Der Klang *(sound)* von Big Ben … ____________

j) Die Linien *(lines)* der U-Bahn *(tube)* … ____________

k) Die Türme *(towers)* des Towers … ____________

Info plus

The Tower of London

Der *Tower of London* ist nicht - wie der Name vermuten lässt - ein einzelner Turm, sondern ein festungsartiger Bau an der Themse. Sein Bau wurde unter Wilhelm dem Eroberer ***(William the Conqueror)*** 1078 begonnen. Der Tower war Festung, Waffenkammer, Palast, Gefängnis, Sitz der englischen Münzherstellung, Staatsarchiv und Observatorium für die Himmelsbeobachtung. Viele englische Könige und Königinnen wohnten zeitweise dort und vor einer Krönung war es Tradition für den Monarchen oder die Monarchin, im Tower zu übernachten. Heute ist der Tower berühmt, weil man in ihm die britischen Kronjuwelen bestaunen kann, die zu den größten und wertvollsten der Welt gehören.

13 Bilde mit jedem Bild einen *of*-Genitiv.

a) bells

b) owner (Besitzer)

c) price

d) saddle

e) TV set (age) How old?

f) height?

g) roof huts (Hütten) h) mountain top

a) ______________________ b) ______________________

c) ______________________ d) ______________________

e) ______________________ f) ______________________

g) ______________________ h) ______________________

1.8 *this – that – these – those*

Regel

Demonstrativpronomen

+ ***this***, ***that***, ***these*** und ***those*** sind sogenannte Demonstrativpronomen. Sie werden in den folgenden Bedeutungen verwendet:

this	these
Singular	Plural
diese, dieser, dieses (dies)	diese (dies) (hier)
(gedachtes) Bezugswort: hier/here	

that	those
Singular	Plural
der, die, das jener, jene, jenes	diese, jene (dort)
(gedachtes) Bezugswort: dort/there	

+ ***This*** und ***these*** beziehen sich auf Personen oder Dinge, die sich **nahe** am Sprechenden befinden (oft auch angezeigt durch *here*).
+ ***That*** und ***those*** beziehen sich auf Personen oder Dinge, die **weiter entfernt** sind (oft auch angezeigt durch *over there* = *da drüben/dort*).

14 Füge *this is*, *these are*, *that is* oder *those are* ein.

a) ____________ terrible pictures, but ____________ wonderful posters.

b) ____________ a nice car, but ____________ an ugly old camper.

c) ____________ here a new bike? – No, but ____________ a new one over there.

d) ____________ cheap pencils? – Yes, and ____________ cheap pencils over there, too.

15 Deine Austauschpartnerin Julia aus Schottland ist bei dir angekommen. Sie zeigt dir ein Foto ihrer Familie. Fülle die Lücken.

Julia says:

"_____________ people here are my parents, and _____________ boys over there are my brothers."

"_____________ building here is my parents' house, and _____________ house over there is our neighbours' house."

"_____________ person on the right is my grandma. _____________ person here next to her is my grandpa."

"_____________ cat over there is Sally."

"And _____________ dog here is our dog Barkey. Barkey likes Sally, but Sally doesn't like Barkey."

"_____________ over there is our neighbours' horse. His name is Fury."

"And _____________ tree over there is his favourite apple tree. Fury likes to eat

_____________ apples over there."

1.9 Übersicht der Pronomen

Regel

Pronomen im Überblick

Die folgende Übersicht zeigt dir verschiedene Pronomen.

Person	Subjektfall	Objektfall	possessiv	demonstrativ
1. P. Singular	**I** - ich	**me** - mir, mich	**my** - mein, meine	
2. P. Singular	**you** - du	**you** - dir, dich	**your** - dein, deine	
3. P. Singular	**he/she/it** - er, sie, es	**him** - ihm, ihn **her** - ihr, sie **it** - ihm, es	**his** - sein, seine **her** - ihr, ihre **its** - sein, seine	**this, that**
1. P. Plural	**we** - wir	**us** - uns	**our** - unser, unsere	
2. P. Plural	**you** - ihr	**you** - euch	**your** - euer, euere	
3. P. Plural	**they** - sie	**them** - ihnen, sie	**their** - ihr, ihre	**these, those**

Regel

Befehlsformen und Verbote

+ Man kann **Befehlsformen** ganz einfach nach folgendem Muster erstellen:

Verb in der Grundform + **evtl. Objekt(e)**

Beispiele: *Read the book. Give me the pencil-case. Sit down. Open the window. Close the door. Tell me the story. Wash the car. Tidy up your room.*

+ Verneinte Befehlsformen **(Verbote)** bildet man so:

Don't + **Verb in der Grundform** + **evtl. Objekt(e)**

Beispiele: *Don't give her the book. Don't tell me the story. Don't ask them this question. Don't pay him the money. Don't stand on the table.*

16 Übersetze und verwende das passende Objektpronomen.

a) Gib mir bitte das Buch. ______________________

b) Erzähle ihm die Geschichte nicht. ______________________

c) Schreibe ihr einen Brief. ______________________

d) Lege es (das Heft) auf den Tisch. ______________________

17 Setze das richtige Pronomen ein.

a) Look, Dorothee is in ________ room. ________'s happy. ________ neighbours are in ________ garden. ________'re very happy, too.

b) Steve is thirteen. ________'s not twelve. ________'s looking at ________. ________'m his friend. ________ bike is new, ________ like ________ very much.

c) Jane: "Fred and his sister are at home this afternoon. Can ________ please call ________ at five o'clock?" – Dan: "Yes, ________ can. But ________ must first do ________ homework."

d) "Don't touch ________, Pete. ________'m in a bad mood (Stimmung)."

e) ________ parents are in ________ garage. ________'re washing ________ car.

1.10 *There is* ... und *There are* ...

Regel

***There is* ... und *There are* ...**

Für die deutsche umgangssprachliche Wendung „**Es gibt** ..." wird im Englischen oft „***There is*** ..." (Singular) und „***There are*** ..." (Plural) verwendet:
„Am Samstag gibt es eine Party." ➞ "There is a party on Saturday."
„In München gibt es viele Brauereien." ➞ "There are many breweries in Munich."

Manchmal sind im Deutschen auch die Übersetzungen mit *„Da ist ..."* und *„Da sind ..."* angebracht, zum Beispiel bei: *"There are many pens on the desk."*

18 Bilde einen Satz mit *There is, There are, Is there* oder *Are there.*

a) Ist Käse im Kühlschrank? ________________

b) In Berlin gibt es einen berühmten *(famous)* Fernsehturm *(TV tower).*

____

c) Auf dem Tisch liegen sechs Bleistifte. ________________

d) Es gibt viele *(many)* Probleme. ________________

Tipp

Ähnlich klingende Wörter

Achtung, diese Wörter klingen ähnlich und können leicht verwechselt werden, wenn man beim Hören nicht ihre Bedeutungen begreift.

there	bedeutet immer *da/dort* oder zusammen mit *is* und *are* → *es gibt*
they're	Kurzform von *they are* (deutsch: *sie sind)*
their	Possessivpronomen, 3. Person Plural (deutsch: *ihr/ihre)*
your	Possessivpronomen, 2. Person Singular und Plural (deutsch: *dein/deine*, *euer/eure* oder *Ihr/Ihre* als Höflichkeitsform bzw. Sie-Anrede)
you're	Kurzform von *you are* (deutsch: *du bist / Sie sind / ihr seid)*
it's	Kurzform von *it is* (deutsch: *es ist)*
its	Possessivpronomen, 3. Person Singular sächlich (deutsch: *sein/seine)*
his	Possessivpronomen. 3. Person Singular männlich (deutsch: *sein/seine)*
he's	Kurzform von *he is* (deutsch*: er ist)*

19 Setze ein: *there's – they're – their – your – you're – it's – its – his – he's.*

a) ______ Monday morning. Paul is in ______ classroom. So ______ not at home.

b) Mary: "Look, ______ a black cat over there on the wall. Is that ______ cat, Dan?"

c) Sally: "You aren't fifteen, ______ twelve, Sam."

d) Pam: "This is our house. ______ very old, but ______ windows are new."

e) Susan: "My friends' parents are from Ireland. ______ not from Scotland".

f) Bill: "My uncle Tim's children are interested in sports. ______ favourite sport is basketball."

g) Jack: "Let's go swimming." - Stan: "Oh no, ______ too hot today."

h) Willy's not good at Maths, but ______ excellent at Biology.

i) ______ too late to go out for dinner.

1.11 *have got*

Regel

Verwendung von *have got*

Konstruktionen mit *have got* kann man immer dann verwenden, wenn man nach dem **Eigentum/Besitz einer Person** fragt oder darüber spricht:

Er hat ein neues Skateboard. → *He* ***has got*** *a new skateboard.* (*He****'s got*** *a new …*)

Ihr habt fünf Minuten Zeit. → *You* ***have got*** *(You****'ve got****) five minutes.*

Habt ihr Probleme? → ***Have*** *you* ***got*** *problems?*

Hat sie blaue Ohrringe? → ***Has*** *she* ***got*** *blue earrings?*

Die Formen von *have got* in Aussagesätzen und in Fragesätzen lauten:

Aussagesatz	Kurzform	Fragesatz
I have got …	I've got …	Have I got … ?
You have got …	You've got …	Have you got …?
He/She/It has got …	He's/She's/It's got …	Has he/she/it got … ?
We have got …	We've got …	Have we got … ?
You have got …	You've got …	Have you got … ?
They have got …	They've got …	Have they got … ?

20 Übersetze.

a) Mein Bruder hat zwei Vögel. ______

b) Hat er seine Hefte zuhause? ______

c) Hast du meinen Bleistift? ______

d) Haben deine Eltern zwei Autos? ______

Regel

Verneinung von *have got* und Kurzantworten

- Die Formen der **Verneinung** lauten immer ***have not got*** (Kurzform: ***haven't got***). In der 3. Person Singular lautet sie ***has not got*** (Kurzform: ***hasn't got***).
- Auf **Fragen** mit *have got* gibst du folgende **Kurzantworten**:
  Have you got a dog? – Yes, I ***have****./No, I* ***haven't****.*
  So funktioniert das immer, mit Ausnahme der 3. Person Singular:
  Has *he/she/it* ***got*** *…? – Yes, he/she/it* ***has****./No, he/she/it* ***hasn't****.*

21 Verneine jeden Satz.

a) He's got much time. ______

b) Have you got a sister? ______

c) They've got a tree in their garden. ______

d) My aunt's got a big family. ______

22 Gib die passende Kurzantwort.

a) Have they got much money? - No, ______.

b) Hasn't Mary got a headache? - Yes, ______.

c) Have you got time for me? - No, ______.

d) Have his parents got twins? - Yes, ______.

1.12 Grundlagen der Satzstellung im Aussagesatz

Regel

S - P - O im Aussagesatz

Im englischen Aussagesatz lautet die Satzstruktur immer:
Subjekt - Prädikat (Verb) - Objekt.

I know a lot of jokes. → *Ich kenne viele Witze.*

23 Bilde einfache Aussagesätze nach der Regel S-P-O. Schreibe in dein Heft.

1 Wie fragt man nach dem Objekt eines Satzes? ______________________

2 Wie lauten die englischen Pronomen im Subjekt- und im Objektfall?

Subjektfall: ____

Objektfall: ____

3 Wie heißen die verneinten Kurzformen von *be*?

____

4 Wie unterscheiden sich *they're* und *their* bzw. *he's* und *his*?

____

____

5 Welchen Genitiv verwendet man, wenn das Bezugswort eine Person ist bzw. mehrere Personen sind?

____

6 Worin besteht der Unterschied zwischen *these* und *those*?

____

7 Wie kann man *there is* und *there are* meist ins Deutsche übersetzen?

____

8 Wann kann man Formen von *have got* verwenden?

____

9 Wie heißt die verneinte Form von *have got*? ______________________

10 Wie lautet die Satzstellung in englischen Aussagesätzen?

____

1 Übersetze. Verwende die entsprechende Form von *be*, wenn möglich in der Kurzform. ___/16

Mike ist der Hamster *(hamster)* meiner Schwester. Er ist zwei Jahre alt. Seine Ohren sind weiß und seine Augen sind braun. Ist er ein „Junge" oder ein „Mädchen"? Er ist ein männlicher *(male)* Hamster. Meine Schwester ist sehr glücklich mit Mike. Sie ist ein Tierfreund *(pet lover)*. Sie ist auch sehr an Katzen interessiert *(interested in)*.

____

____

____

____

____

____

____

2 Füge das passende Pronomen ein. ___/10

_______ uncle is an English teacher. The name of _______ school is Barton Comprehensive. _______ likes English ghost stories very much. _______ like adventure stories. _______ favourite subjects at school are Maths and Arts. _______ Arts teacher is a wonderful man. _______'s young and _______ lessons are so interesting. I like _______ and he likes _______.

mein - seine
er
ich - meine
unser
er - seine
ihn - mich

3 Verneine jeden Satz. Verwende Kurzformen. ___/5

a) I'm lazy. _______________

b) She's ten. _______________

c) Is he tall? _______________

d) Are we poor? _______________

e) They are at school. _______________

__/5 **4** Die neuen Nachbarn sind sehr neugierig und stellen viele Fragen. Bilde die entsprechende Kurzantwort.

a) Has your mother really got five sisters and two brothers? – Yes, ______________.

b) Is Mr Dexter your mother's brother? – No, ______________.

c) Have Mr and Mrs Miller got a cottage *(Landhaus)*? – No, ______________.

d) Are they in England at the moment? – Yes, ______________.

e) Are you ill today? – No, ______________.

__/5 **5** Füge den passenden Genitiv ein.

a) Our ______________ hobby is very expensive. *(der Kinder)*

b) The ______________ is brand new. *(Lampe meines Fahrrads)*

c) Peter ______________ goldfish is over eight years old.

d) ______________ car is a 1999 Chevrolet. *(meiner Eltern)*

e) He likes ______________. *(Farbe unseres Hauses)*

__/20 **6** Bilde Befehlssätze.

a) Schlagt eure Bücher auf. ______________

b) Sprich nicht während des Unterrichts. ______________

c) Sarah, hilf ihm! ______________

d) Sagt das noch einmal *(again)*. ______________

e) Mache jetzt nicht deine Hausaufgaben. ______________

f) Gib mir die schwere *(heavy)* Tasche. ______________

g) Setze dich hin. ______________

h) Schaue nicht deinen Nachbarn an. ______________

i) Lege das Federmäppchen auf den Tisch. ______________

j) Schlafe nicht. ______________

7 Finde den oder die Fehler, streiche den fehlerhaften Teil durch und verbessere jeden Satz in der Leerzeile. ___/6

a) There's so many nice pupils in our new class.

____

b) Have your mum got much time for her hobbies?

____

c) The young girl likes he's fathers new DVDs.

____

d) He is'nt interested in football. He likes he's basketball team.

____

e) Its Saturday afternoon and their's the news on TV.

____

f) Look at this people. Their really nasty.

____

8 Setze die genannte Sprechsituation ins Englische um. ___/10

a) Frage deine Freundin Sue, ob sie Geld für eine neue CD hat.

____

b) Fordere deinen Freund Pete auf, die Fenster und die Türen zu schließen.

____

c) Teile Herrn Lewis mit, dass du nicht Schüler an der Schule deines Vaters bist.

____

d) Verbiete Jack, dich „Esel" *(donkey)* zu nennen.

____

e) Frage Jim, ob seine Schwester die Masern *(the measles)* hat.

____

Gesamtpunktzahl ____/77

2 Verben: Zeitformen der Gegenwart

Wenn wir im Deutschen ausdrücken wollen, ob etwas ganz allgemein in der Gegenwart oder gerade in diesem Augenblick stattfindet, tun wir dies mit Ergänzungen wie „im Augenblick" oder „im Moment". Im Englischen gibt es im Gegensatz zum Deutschen sogar eine spezielle Zeitform, die ausdrückt, dass etwas im Augenblick stattfindet.

2.1 *Simple present:* Die einfache Form des Präsens

Regel

Bildung des *simple present*

- Die einfache Form des Präsens *(simple present)* hat die gleiche Form wie der Infinitiv, d. h. die Grundform des Verbs.
  play: I play, you play (du spielst), we play, you play (ihr spielt), they play
- Nur in der **dritten Person Singular im *simple present*** wird ein **-s** angehängt.
  play: he plays, she plays, it plays
- Bei Verben, die auf einen **Zischlaut** enden, wird in der dritten Person Singular **-es** angehängt *(he watches, she kisses).*
- Bei Verben, die auf **Konsonant und -y** enden, wird in der dritten Person Singular y zu **-ies** *(hurry: she hurries, carry: he carries;* ***aber:*** *buy: he buys).*
- Die dritte Person Singular der Verben ***go*** und ***do*** endet im *simple present* ebenfalls auf **-es** *(He often goes to his friend. She never does her homework.).*

1 Bilde die entsprechende Form im *simple present*.

	play	write	put	buy	watch	hurry
I						
you						
he, she, it						
we						
you						
they						

2 Schreibe die entsprechende Form des *simple present* in jede Lücke.

On schooldays I ____________ (get up) at seven o'clock. Then I ____________ (go) to the bathroom and ____________ (wash) myself.
My brother ____________ (get up) later. His school ____________ (start) at nine.
My sister ____________ (be) also still in bed.
She ____________ (go) to university and often ____________ (work) very late. After breakfast, I ____________ (brush) my teeth and then I ____________ (take) the number 8 bus to school. My friends Tom and Trish usually ____________ (wait) for me in front of the school.
They ________ (be) brother and sister.

Regel

Verwendung des *simple present*

- Das *simple present* wird verwendet, wenn etwas **immer wieder** so geschieht oder immer wieder so ist: *Mike always goes to school at 8.30. (Er tat dies gestern, tut dies heute und wird es in Zukunft auch tun.)*
- Auch wenn **Handlungen neu einsetzen** oder unmittelbar neue Vorgänge folgen, wird das *simple present* verwendet: *Suddenly the doorbell rings and Mike runs downstairs.*
- Die **Satzstellung S-P-O** (Subjekt - Prädikat/Verb - Objekt) muss grundsätzlich eingehalten werden!
- **Häufigkeitsadverbien** wie *always, never* und *often* sind Signalwörter und müssen **vor dem Verb** stehen: *She always goes to bed very late. He never watches TV in the morning.*

Tipp

Signalwörter

Wenn du unsicher bist, welche Zeitform du wählen musst, können sogenannte Signalwörter weiterhelfen. Die Signalwörter des *simple present* sind z.B. ***always*** *(immer)*, ***often*** (oft), ***sometimes*** (manchmal), ***seldom*** (selten), ***never*** (nie), ***every day*****/*****week*****/*****year*****/*****holiday*****/*****afternoon*****/*****Tuesday*** usw.

3 Setze die entsprechende Verbform in die Lücke ein.

Every Sunday Bianca ____________ (get up) late. After breakfast, she ____________ (take) a shower and then she ____________ (sit) down in the living room and ____________ (watch) a show on TV. Then she ____________ (help) her mom in the kitchen. She ____________ (put) forks, knives and plates on the table and ____________ (fetch) some wine for her father from the cellar. In the afternoon, Bianca and her parents ____________ (go) for a walk to the park or, if the weather ______ (be) bad, they ____________ (play) 'Settlers of Catan'. Sometimes they also ____________ (have) visitors. Bianca's grandpa sometimes ____________ (come) for tea.

He usually ____________ (bring) a cake. Bianca ____________ (call) it "The best cake in the world!".

In the evening, Bianca ____________ (do) her homework and later she ____________ (watch) TV or ____________ (read) a book. She usually ____________ (go) to bed at nine o'clock because she ____________ (get up) very early on school-days.

She ____________ (live) in a small village and ____________ (take) the bus to school. The bus ____________ (leave) every morning at seven o'clock!

Info plus

Wichtige Verbkonstruktionen für den Tagesablauf

to get up – aufstehen
to brush one's teeth – Zähne putzen
to have breakfast – frühstücken
to prepare a meal – ein Essen zubereiten
to watch TV – fernsehen
to do one's homework – seine Hausaufgaben machen
to take a shower – duschen
to sit down – sich hinsetzen
to go to school – in die Schule gehen
to go for a walk – spazieren gehen
to go to bed – ins Bett gehen

Regel

Verneinung des *simple present*

Im *simple present* verneinst du mit ***do not*** (Kurzform: ***don't***) bzw. in der dritten Person Singular mit ***does not*** (Kurzform: ***doesn't***).

*I **don't** speak English. You **don't** speak Italian. He/She **doesn't** read a lot. It **doesn't** rain. We **don't** know the story. You **don't** have a chance. **Don't** they like tea?*

4 Die Schule in Großbritannien unterscheidet sich von der Schule in Deutschland. Lies dir den Text über englische Schulen durch und bilde dann verneinte Sätze über das deutsche Schulsystem.

Typically, school starts at 8.45. Pupils have assembly *(Versammlung)* in the morning. Lessons last for 50 minutes. After four lessons pupils go to lunch to the school cafeteria. Every afternoon English pupils sit for two more lessons in school. School usually ends at 3.15. Then the pupils do their homework.

In Germany, school ____________________

Pupils ____________________

Lessons ____________________

After four lessons, ____________________

German pupils ____________________ every afternoon.

School in Germany usually ____________________

German pupils ____________________. But you do!

5 *A teenage tragedy.* Bilde verneinte Sätze.

a) He lies to her. ____________________

b) She believes him. ____________________

c) "Do you miss me?" ____________________

d) "I love you!" ____________________

e) "He has another girlfriend." ____________________

f) "I like him!" ____________________

g) He leaves her. ____________________

h) She forgets him. ____________________

Regel

Fragebildung im *simple present*

- Auch einige **Fragen** müssen **mit *do/does*** gebildet werden.
  Do *I like ice cream?* ***Do*** *you like pop music?* ***Does*** *he/she/it love pizza?*
  Do *we hate yoghurt?* ***Do*** *you do your homework?* ***Do*** *they go for a walk?*
- Bei Entscheidungsfragen heißt die **Kurzantwort** (das deutsche „Ja" oder „Nein"): *Yes, I /you/we/you/they* ***do****. Yes, he/she/it* ***does****.*
  No, I/you/we/you/they ***don't****. No, he/she/it* ***doesn't****.*
- Fragen mit Fragewörtern bildet man nach dem gleichen Muster:
  Where do you come from? What does he do?
- Ist das Fragewort *Who* das Subjekt des Satzes, erfolgt keine Umschreibung mit *do*: *Who likes to have a cup of tea?* **Aber:** *Who* ***does*** *he always meet in the afternoons?* (Hier fragt das Fragewort nach dem Objekt!)

6 Bilde zunächst die Frage, dann die positive (+) oder negative (–) Antwort.

a) My father works in the garden every weekend. (+) ______________________

____

____

b) My father helps in the kitchen whenever he can. (-) ______________________

____

____

c) Tom and Linda play tennis every afternoon. (+) ______________________

____

____

d) They don't do their homework. (-) ______________________

____

____

e) We read comics in the morning. (-) ______________________

____

____

Info plus Sprachen arbeiten oft mit Bildern. Manchmal ähneln die englischen **Sprachbilder** den deutschen, manchmal tun sie dies nicht.

It's raining cats and dogs.	*Es schüttet aus Eimern.*
A bird in the hand is worth two in the bush.	*Der Spatz in der Hand ist besser als die Taube auf dem Dach.*
Don't throw the baby out with the bathwater.	*Schütte das Baby nicht mit dem Badewasser aus.* (Als es noch keine Zentralheizung gab, wurde nur selten gebadet. Der Vater durfte als erster ins Wasser, die Kinder badeten als letzte!)

7 Lies den Text und bilde anschließend Fragen.

Today it's raining cats and dogs. As on every Sunday, Bianca gets up late. After breakfast, she takes a shower and then she sits down in the living room and watches a show on TV. Then she helps her mom in the kitchen. She puts forks, knives and plates on the table and fetches some wine for her father from the cellar. In the afternoon, Bianca and her parents go for a walk to the park. When the weather is bad, they play 'Settlers of Catan'. Sometimes they also have visitors. Bianca's grandpa sometimes comes for tea. He usually brings a cake. Bianca calls it, "The best cake in the world!". In the evening, Bianca does her homework and later she watches TV or reads a book. She usually goes to bed at nine o'clock because she gets up very early on schooldays. She lives in a small village and takes the bus to school. The bus leaves at seven o'clock every morning!

a) When ______________________ every Sunday?

b) When ______________________ a shower?

c) What ______________________ after her shower?

d) What ______________________ on the table?

e) Where ______________________ for a walk?

f) When ______________________ 'Settlers of Catan'?

g) Who ______________________ for tea sometimes?

h) What ______________________ call it?

i) When ______________________ her homework on Sundays?

j) When ______________________________ to bed?

k) Why ______________________________ to bed at nine o'clock?

l) Where ______________________________ live?

m) How ______________________________ get to school?

n) When ______________________________ every morning?

Our questions:

o) What ______ you think about this exercise?

p) What ______ you ______ to improve your English? (*improve* = verbessern)

q) What ______ we say? – Yes, we say "Well done!" (*Well done!* = Gut gemacht!)

8 Finde die passende Frage. Frage nach dem unterstrichenen Teil.

a) ______________________________

Tom and Mike are in town.

b) ______________________________

Tanja is Jenny's German friend.

c) ______________________________

Yes, my parents have got a TV in their bedroom.

d) ______________________________

No, there is no toilet downstairs.

e) ______________________________

I'm eleven years old.

Tipp

Fragewörter im Überblick

Who? – Wer? Wen? Wem?

What? – Was?

Where? – Wo?

Why? – Warum? Weshalb?

How many? – Wie viele? (zählbar)

How many cars are there in the street?

Wie viele Autos sind auf der Straße?

Whose? – Wessen?

Who's? *(Who is?)* – Wer ist?

When? – Wann?

How? – Wie?

How much? – Wie viel? (nicht zählbar)

How much milk is in the fridge?

Wie viel Milch ist im Kühlschrank?

Regel

Fragen mit *why*

Auf *Why*-Fragen wird mit *because* (weil) geantwortet. Beginne eine Antwort im geschriebenen Englisch aber immer mit dem Hauptsatz, nie mit *because*.
Beispiel: *Why does Bianca like her grandpa? - She likes her grandpa because he always brings a cake.*

2.2 *Present progressive:* Die Verlaufsform des Präsens

Regel

Bildung des *present progressive*

- Die Verlaufsform der Gegenwart, das *present progressive*, bildet man mit der **-*ing*-Form des Verbs** und der entsprechenden **Form von *be***.
  *I **am** eating. You **are** reading. He/She/It **is** drinking. We **are** waiting. You **are** walking. They **are** playing.*
- Die *-ing*-Form bildet man, indem man ***-ing* an die Grundform des Verbs** (Infinitiv) anhängt:
  eat → eating, stand → standing, play → playing,
  wait → waiting
- Verneint wird durch ***am not, are not, is not*** und deren Kurzformen ***aren't*** und ***isn't***.
- Sonderfälle:

sit → sitting *run → running* *hit → hitting*	+ Konsonant	Nach einem kurzen, einfachen und betonten Selbstlaut (Vokal) wird der Mitlaut am Ende des Wortes (Endkonsonant) verdoppelt.
make → making *take → taking* *leave → leaving*	-e	Wird ein e am Ende eines Wortes nicht gesprochen, so fällt es im *present progressive* weg.

9 Bilde jeweils einen Aussagesatz mit dem *present progressive*.

a) come He ______________________ home.

b) clean They ______________________ their rooms.

c) shut She ______________ the window.

d) talk We ______________ much at the moment.

e) put He ______________ the pen on the desk.

f) read You ______________ the newspaper.

g) write She ______________ a letter to her friend.

h) get It ______________ hot.

i) buy I ______________ a new bike.

Regel

Verwendung des *present progressive*

- Das *present progressive* wird verwendet, wenn eine **Handlung gerade stattfindet**.
- Das *present progressive* wird verwendet, wenn im Deutschen **„im Augenblick", „im Moment", „jetzt"** oder **„gerade"** dastehen könnte.
- **Signalwörter** für das *present progressive* sind z. B. *at the moment* oder *now*.

10 Im Park. Beschreibe, was die Leute auf dem Bild gerade tun.

A man ______________ (sit) on a bench. He ______________ (read) a newspaper. A dog ______________ (sniff) at the man's leg.

Two girls ______________________ (ride) their bikes.

They ______________________ (laugh) about the man. A bird ____________

(fly) in the air. Another bird ______________________________ (sing) in a tree.

A little girl ______________________ (have) an ice cream.

A boy ______________________ (stand) next to her. He wants an ice cream,

too, so he ______________________ (pull) at his mother's arm. The boy's

mother __________________________________ (talk) to another woman.

The two women __________________________________ (smile).

2.3 *Present progressive* und *simple present*

Regel

Die Präsensformen im Vergleich

present progressive **(Verlaufsform)**	***simple present*** **(einfache Form)**
Look, Jane ***is writing*** *a letter to her friend.* *He* ***is living*** *in New York at the moment.*	*She* ***writes*** *a letter every week.* *He* ***lives*** *in New York.*
• Handlungen, die im Augenblick ablaufen • Zustände, die gerade so sind	• Handlungen, die immer so geschehen • Zustände, die immer so sind • Handlungen, die neu einsetzen • Vorgänge, die aufeinander folgen

11 Setze die korrekte Form des Verbs und das Adverb an der richtigen Stelle ein.

Two teachers are watching the children during the break.

Mr D.: "Look at the children. It's like every year."

Mrs R.: "Yes, Mike __________________________________ (sit) alone over there.

He __________________________________ (never, play) with the boys."

Mr D.: "And Julia and Hanna ____________________ (talk).

They ______________________ (usually, talk) a lot."

Mrs R.: "And Elly ______ (come back) from the toilet.

She ______ (go to the toilet; every lesson).

But Sandy ______ (never, sit) alone, only sometimes.

But then, she ______ (always, have got) trouble with her boyfriend. Poor girl!"

12 *A special day.* Übersetze.

a) Jeden Freitag nach der Arbeit geht Mike in eine Snackbar. (jeden Freitag = *every Friday*)

______

b) Dann isst er ein belegtes Brot. (dann = *then*; belegtes Brot = *sandwich*)

______

c) (Gerade) kommt Sandra. Sie lächelt.

______

d) Sie ist glücklich, weil heute ein besonderer Tag ist. (besonderer = *special*)

______

e) Mike nimmt Sandra gewöhnlich in seinem Auto mit nach Hause.

______

f) Heute bleiben sie bis neun Uhr abends (am Abend) in der Stadt, weil heute Sandras Geburtstag ist. (bleiben = *stay*; bis = *until*)

______

______

g) Sie gehen ins Kino und schauen einen Film mit Leonardo di Caprio an. (zuerst = *first*)

______

______

h) Sie gehen nicht in die Disco.

______

11 Wann gebraucht man im Englischen das *simple present*?

____

12 Welche Zeitform beschreibt, dass eine Handlung gerade abläuft?

____

13 Welche Zeitform des Präsens zeigt das Signalwort *usually* an?

____

14 Welche Zeitform zeigt das Signalwort *now* an? ______________

15 Ergänze den Reim zum *simple present*: *He, she, it,* das ____ muss mit!

16 Nenne mindestens drei Signalwörter des *simple present*.

____

17 Wie enden Verben, deren Endung aus einem Konsonanten und *y* bestehen, in der 3. Person des *simple present*? ______________

18 Bilde die 3. Person Singular der Verben *go, do* und *buy* im *simple present*.

____

19 Wie lautet die Verneinung von *have got* in der 3. Person Singular?

____

20 Mit welchem deutschen Zusatzwort wird das *present progressive* oft übersetzt? ______________

21 Wie lautet die Reihenfolge der Satzglieder im englischen Aussagesatz? Unterscheidet sie sich dabei vom deutschen Aussagesatz?

____

____

___/15 **1** *Present progressive* oder *simple present*? Welche Zeitform ist hier richtig?

Hello, my name ____________ (be) is Dopey, one of the 7 dwarfs (dwarf = *Zwerg*).

I ____________ ____________ (usually, live) 'Beyond the Seven Hills', but I

________________________ (live) in the Alps at the moment.

I ____________ (go) to work in the goldmine every day, but I

(not work) ____________ at the moment, because I ____________ (be) on

holiday. My friend Grumpy ________________________ (sit) over there.

He ____________ (not feel) happy, so he ________________________

(shout) at Doc. Grumpy ________________________ (always, shout) at us.

I ________________________ ________________________ (never, shout) at

my friends. They all ____________ (like) me but they ________________________ (not like) Grumpy.

___/9 **2** Formuliere die richtige Frage zu jeder Antwort. Frage nach dem unterstrichenen Satzteil.

Dopey is a famous person. A reporter of the "Dwarf News" wants to interview him. You take his part.

a) ____?

I am from 'Beyond the Seven Hills'.

b) ____?

I am 85 years old.

c) ____?

Yes, I've got a cat and a hamster.

d) ____?

Yes, I do. I like singing and laughing.

e) ____?

No, he doesn't. Grumpy hates songs.

f) ____?

I've got one girl friend, Snow White and six "boy" friends.

g) ____ ?

Snow White isn't a dwarf. She's a princess.

h) ____ ?

She lives with us because her stepmother doesn't like her.

3 Übersetze

__/12

a) Ich mag Märchen *(fairy tales)* und ich lese gerade ein Buch über die Brüder Grimm *(about the Brothers Grimm)*.
b) Diese Geschichtenerzähler *(story tellers)* sind in Deutschland sehr beliebt *(popular)*.
c) Jeder *(everybody)* kennt sie. Ihre Geschichten sind spannend *(exciting)* und interessant.
d) In der Schule sprechen wir gerade über Wilhelm Busch.
e) Dieser Autor *(author)* ist berühmt für *(famous for)* seine Gedichte *(poems)* und seine lustigen Reime *(rhymes)*.
f) Viele Menschen kennen seine Geschichten von Max und Moritz.

Gesamtpunktzahl

____/36

3 Verben: Zeitformen der Vergangenheit und Zukunft

earlier → *now* → *later*
Vergangenheit Gegenwart Zukunft

Wenn wir ausdrücken wollen, ob etwas vor oder nach dem Jetzt stattfindet, tun wir dies mit Zeitangaben sowie mit speziellen Formen des Verbs. Die Sätze „Ich bin gegangen." und „Er wird gehen." sagen klar, wann etwas stattfindet. Ganz ähnlich funktioniert das im Englischen.

3.1 *Simple past:* Die einfache Form der Vergangenheit

Regel

Bildung des *simple past*

- **Regelmäßige Verben** bilden die einfache Form der Vergangenheit, das *simple past*, durch Anhängen der Endung **-ed** an die **Grundform des Verbs (Infinitiv)**. Beispiel: *look* → *look**ed**, play* → *play**ed**, jump* → *jump**ed**, watch* → *watch**ed***
- Das *simple past* ist für alle Personen gleich.
  *I look**ed**; you look**ed**; he/she/it look**ed**;*
  *we look**ed**; you look**ed**; they look**ed***
- Beachte die Schreibung:

*wip**e*** → *wip**ed***	stummes **-e**	Wird das **-e** in der Grundform (im Infinitiv) nicht gesprochen (stummes -e), wird es auch im *simple past* nicht gesprochen.
*sto**p*** → *sto**pped***	Endkonsonant nach kurzem Vokal	Nach einem kurzen, einfachen und betonten Selbstlaut (Vokal) wird der **Mitlaut** am Ende des Wortes (Endkonsonant) **verdoppelt**.
*hurr**y*** → *hurr**ied***	**-y** → **-ied**	Geht einem **-y** am Ende eines Verbs in der Grundform (im Infinitiv) ein Konsonant voraus, wird dieses **-y** im *simple past* zu **-ied**.

1 Bilde die einfache Vergangenheit der dieser Verben.

Tina works.		They play.	
We ask.		She answers.	
I watch.		Tom visits.	
They talk.		You want.	
She likes.		He cleans.	
It rains.		I jump.	
I look.		They hurry.	

Regel

Aussprache des *-ed*

- Endet ein Verb in der Grundform stimmhaft, dann wird die Endung *-ed* im *past tense* auch stimmhaft (weich) gesprochen: *stay* → *stayed* [d].
- Endet ein Verb in der Grundform stimmlos, dann wird die Endung *-ed* im *past tense* auch stimmlos (hart) gesprochen: *pick* → *picked* [t]; *stop* → *stopped* [t].
- Endet das Verb mit *-t* oder *-d*, wird die Endung *-ed* als [id] gesprochen: *want* → *wanted* [id]; *wait* → *waited* [id]; *command* → *commanded* [id].

Regel

Das *simple past* von *be*

- Die Formen des *simple past* von *be* (sein) lauten:
  I ***was****; you* ***were****; he/she/it* ***was****; we* ***were****; you* ***were****; they* ***were****.*
- Für die unregelmäßigen Verben *(irregular verbs)* gibt es keine Bildungsregeln. Man muss sie einfach lernen. Siehe hierzu die Seiten 136/137.

2 Übersetze.

a) Ich war krank. ______________________

b) Ihr wart im Urlaub. ______________________

c) Wir waren in der Schule. ______________________

d) Er war hungrig. ______________________

3 Eine Möglichkeit, sich die unregelmäßigen Verben zu merken, besteht darin, diese rhythmisch zu sprechen, zu „rappen". Weil du bald eine dritte Form (Partizip Perfekt) lernen musst, ist es einfacher, diese Formen gleich dazuzulernen.
Rappe den *„Irregular Verbs Rap"* so rhythmisch wie möglich!

Irregular Verbs Rap

Go, went, gone; shine, shone, shone; do, did, done;
take, took, taken; shake, shook, shaken;
vergiss nur nicht: foresake, foresook, forsaken.
Bite, bit, bitten; hide, hid, hidden; ride, rode, ridden;
throw, threw, thrown; know, knew, known; forget, forgot, forgotten -
why do I feel so rotten?

Beat, beat, beaten; drink, drank, drunk;
fall, fell, fallen; shrink, shrank, shrunk;
eat, eat, eaten; sink, sank, sunk -
weiß ich Gott sei Dank!
Drive, drove, driven; give, gave, given; rise, rose, risen -
Lernen ist nicht be…

Think, thought; teach, taught; bring, brought; fight, fought; catch, caught;
sleep, slept; creep, crept; weep, wept -
ich glaub ich bin der Depp.
Pay, paid, paid; sing, sang, sung; lay, laid, laid; ring, rang, rung;
make, made, made; hang, hung, hung -
es gibt viel mehr, doch es dauert nicht mehr lang.

Feel, felt; shut, shut; say, said; cut, cut; hold, held; get, got;
lead, led; feed, fed; sell, sold; tell, told; meet, met -
mehr geht heut einfach net.

Die Verben sind irregulär,
sie sind deshalb nicht populär.
Sie sind wirklich nicht sehr schwer,
doch lernen musst du sie selber.

(Die deutschen Bedeutungen der Verben findest du auf den Seiten 136/137.)

Regel

Verneinung und Fragen im *simple past*

- Wie im *simple present* wird auch im *simple past* mit einer Form von *do* verneint. Im *simple past* ist dies die Form **did not** (Kurzform: **didn't**), auf welche die Grundform des Verbs (Infinitiv) folgt. *Did not* und *didn't* bleiben in allen Personen gleich:
  *He **did not (didn't)** come to breakfast.*
  *They **did not (didn't)** do their homework.*
- Auch Fragen müssen, genauso wie im *simple present*, mit *did* oder *didn't* gebildet werden: *What **did** you have for dinner? Who **did** you meet in town? **Didn't** you have a nice evening?*
- Die Kurzantwort bei Entscheidungsfragen ist *Yes, I/you/he/she/it/we/you/they **did*** bzw. *No, I/you/he/she/it/we/you/they **didn't**.*

4 Setze die folgenden Sätze verneint ins *simple past*.

Every Saturday my grandfather goes for a walk late in the afternoon. After teatime he plays chess with his neighbour and then he listens to the evening news on the radio. After that he helps his wife in the kitchen. He cleans the table and then he goes to bed and reads a book. On Sundays he gets up early and goes to church. At lunchtime he always goes to an Italian restaurant.

Last Saturday ____________________

Regel

Verwendung des *simple past*

- Das *simple past* wird für Handlungen und Zustände verwendet, die **abgeschlossen in der Vergangenheit** liegen:
  When I was young, I loved the Teletubbies.
- Es muss immer verwendet werden, wenn du den **Zeitpunkt in der Vergangenheit** kennst oder bei Fragen mit ***when***:
  When did you see him?

früher	jetzt
yesterday, last week, two days ago, in 1970, in the Middle Ages (Mittelalter), *when Robin Hood lived, 10 000 B.C.*	der Moment, in dem du sprichst

5 Füge die passenden Verbformen im *Simple Past* ein. Achtung, hier tauchen auch unregelmäßige Verben auf! Du findest deren Formen auf den Seiten 136/137.

Yesterday Patrick ____________ (have) an exciting adventure. In the afternoon he ____________ (ride) his bike along Baker Street and ____________ (see) two men in black masks next to the bank.

At once Patrick ____________ (jump) off his bike and ____________ (hide) behind a phone box.

Slowly he ____________ (open) the heavy door of the phone box.

'I just hope they won't notice me', he ____________ (think). 'I must call the police.'

But suddenly the bank robbers ____________ (come) out of the bank.

They ____________ (race) away in their car with screeching tyres. Patrick ____________ (try) to see their number plate OXJ 63.. ? Then he ____________ (hear) the sirens of the police cars. When the four police officers ____________ (get) out of their cars, Patrick ____________ (say): "I ____________ (see) part of their number plate." He ____________ (feel) very proud.

3.2 Die Zukunft: *will-future* und *going to-future*

Regel

Die Verwendung der Futur-Formen

	going to-future	*will-future*
Verwendung	• wenn man ausdrücken will, dass jemand etwas **plant** oder **triftige Gründe/Anzeichen** dafür sprechen, dass etwas eintritt. *I'm **going to** have a party next Monday. (Alles ist vorbereitet.)* *Look at those clouds. It's **going to** rain soon. (Dunkle Wolken nahen.)*	• wenn man **Vorhersagen/ Vermutungen** über die Zukunft äußert, die nicht beeinflussbar sind: *It **will** be cloudy tomorrow.* • steht meist nach *I think …, I' m sure …, I hope …, Maybe …* • wenn man sich schnell entscheidet etwas zu tun. *This bag is heavy. I'**ll** help you.*
Form	Das ***going to-Futur*** wird durch eine Form von ***be*** + ***going to*** + **Grundform des Verbs (Infinitiv)** gebildet: *He **is going to** fly to Rio next week.*	***will*** + **Grundform des Verbs (Infinitiv)**: *He **will help** you.* Kurzformen: *I'll, You'll, He'll, She'll It'll, We'll, You'll, They'll*
Verneinung	Verneint wird die Form von ***be***: *He **isn't** going to fly to Rio.*	Für alle Personen gleich: ***Will not*** oder ***won't*** : *He **will not (won't)** help you.*
Frage	***Are** you **going to** bring a friend?* *Where **are** you **going to** go next?*	***Will** he catch the thief?* *Who **will** win the cup finals?*

6 Fülle die Lücken aus.

going to-future	will-future
I ______________________ play football.	He ________ visit his aunt in London.
She ______________________ go home soon.	You ________ know the story.
We ______________________ win this match.	They ________ tell you everything.
It ______________________ snow.	She ________ phone you.

7 Setze die richtige Form der zukünftigen Handlung ein.

Bianca __________ be thirteen next Friday. She __________ invite all her friends to her house, and hopefully everybody __________ have a lot of fun. They __________ dance to their favourite music, and Bianca's mother __________ prepare some delicious snacks. Bianca' s grandparents (not!) __________ come. The music __________ be much too loud for them. Nobody knows whether the sun __________ shine, that's why Bianca __________ have a party in the garage. There they can be as loud as they like and they (not!) __________ bother any neighbours. Annika and Verena, Bianca's best friends, __________ give her a great birthday present: a concert ticket for her favourite band. The concert __________ be in August. They (not!) __________ go to this concert, as they aren't too fond of 'Green Day' themselves.

3.3 Hilfsverben

Regel

Modale Hilfsverben

- Modale Hilfsverben *(modal auxiliaries)* erfüllen nicht die volle Funktion eines Verbs. Sie geben an, **was man kann, darf, muss oder soll oder nicht** kann/darf/muss/soll. Dementsprechend müssen modale Hilfsverben **immer von einem Verb begleitet** werden.
  Vorsicht: dt.: *Ich **kann** Englisch.* → engl.: *I **can speak** English.*
- Modale Hilfsverben verändern ihre Form im Präsens nicht.

Modale Hilfsverben im Überblick

engl. Hilfsverb	Verwendung	deutsch – englisch
+ can **– cannot/can't**	**Fähigkeit**, etwas zu tun/nicht zu tun	*Er kann nicht schwimmen. –* *He **can't** swim.*
+ can **– cannot/can't**	**Erlaubnis** (meist in einer Frage)	*Kann/darf ich das Fenster aufmachen? – **Can/May** I open the window, please?*
+ must **– doesn't/don't have to**	**Notwendigkeit**	*Er muss sein Kaninchen füttern. –* *He **must** feed his rabbit.*
+ have to **– don't/doesn't/didn't have to**	**Ersatzform von *must*,** wenn andere Zeiten als das Präsens gebildet werden müssen	*Er musste Hausaufgaben machen, als er Fußball spielen wollte. –* *He **had to** do his homework when he wanted to play football.* *Er musste nicht früh ins Bett gehen.* *He **didn't have to** go to bed early.*
mustn't	**Verbot**	*Du darfst nicht mit Fremden reden.* *– You **mustn't** talk to strangers.*
needn't	**fehlende Notwendigkeit**	*Du brauchst/musst dich nicht über deinen kleinen Bruder beklagen. Du hast ihn zuerst gezwickt. –* *You **needn't** complain about your little brother. You pinched him first.*

Tipp

- ***Must not/mustn't*** bedeutet nie „nicht müssen", sondern immer **„nicht dürfen"**!
- **„Nicht müssen/brauchen"** wird nie mit *must not/mustn't*, sondern mit ***need not*** übersetzt!

8 Schreibe die richtigen Hilfsverben in die Lücken.

Bianca: "Mum, ______________ to Verena's home?"	I, go
Mother: "Sorry, Bianca, I'm on the telephone. ______________ me later?"	you, ask
Bianca: "But, Mum, I ______________ her about my homework! If I don't go now , she …"	ask
Mother: "I told you I'm on the phone. I will have time for you in a minute. You ______________ at me!"	shout
Bianca: "Oh, Mum, ______________ to your friend later?"	not, talk
Mother: "That's it, Bianca. I told you you ______________ me	disturb
on the phone. So you ______________ to Verena's	go
home today. You ______________ her about your homework."	call
Bianca: "But I ______________! You started your call two hours ago!"	call

9 Bilde Sätze und notiere sie in dein Heft.

Bianca hat Hausarrest bekommen (*She was grounded.*). Jetzt hat sie eine Liste mit Anweisungen bekommen, was sie tun soll oder nicht tun darf.

do her homework alone; call her friends; not leave the house; go to bed early; watch TV; read all the time; beat her little brother; clean the table; wash the dishes; learn the vocabulary

1) Bianca was grounded. Now she has to do her homework alone.

2) …

22 Wie heißen Hilfsverben auf Englisch? ______

23 Nenne drei Beispiele für englische Hilfsverben. ______

24 Wodurch unterscheiden sich Hilfsverben von normalen Verben?

______

25 Welche Endung haben regelmäßige Verben im *simple past*? ______

26 Welchen Unterschied gibt es bei der Bildung der 1. Person Singular und 1. Person Plural im *simple past*?

______

27 Wann wird das *simple past* verwendet?

______

28 Wie wird das *simple past* gebildet, wenn das Verb auf Konsonant + *y* endet? ______

29 Bilde das *simple past* der Verben *take, go, drive*.

______

30 Was ist bei der Aussprache des *-ed* zu beachten, wenn Verben in der Grundform (Infinitiv) auf *t* oder *d* enden? ______

31 Nenne die Formen des *simple past* von *be* (alle Personen).

______

32 Wie heißt die Verneinung von *must*? (Es gibt zwei Möglichkeiten.)

______

__/3

1 Setze das richtige Hilfsverb ein: *can – may – must/have to*

a) Tim: "____________ I feed the cat, please?"

b) Mother: "No, but you ____________ wash the dishes."

c) Tim: "Why ____________ I always do the dirty work?"

__/6

2 *going to-Futur* oder *will-Futur*: Was stimmt?

Bianca's grandpa ____________ (be) 86 soon. He ________________________ (have) a super party on his birthday. He ____________ (invite) Bianca, her parents and all his other friends. He hopes they ________________________ (come) to his party. He ____________ (bake) a big cake for his guests.

But he ________________________ (not invite) his neighbour.

__/27

3 *Grumpy, Snow White* und die Zwerge kennst du bereits. Verwende alle bisher gelernten Zeiten und Hilfsverben.

One day, when Grumpy and his friends ____________ (come) home from the mines they ____________ (find) their house in a terrible mess. They ____________ (go) upstairs and then they ____________ (see) it. Dopey ____________ (ask), "Who ____________ *(sleep)* in my bed?" "I ________________________ (hit) the person very hard!", ____________ (say) Grumpy. He and Doc ____________ (be) angry because their food ____________ (be) gone. But then Snow White ____________________ (live) with the dwarfs, and they all ______________ (fall) in love with her. But they ____________ (warn) her. "Your evil stepmother ______________________ (not like) you. She ____________ (put) on a disguise and ____________________ (try) to kill you, Snow White. You ____________________ (be) very careful!", they ______ (say). And so it __________________ (happen). Twice the dwarfs ____________ (find) her on time, but the third time they ____________ (be) late. When they ______________________ (come) home, Doc ____________ (ask), "Snow White, where ____________ (be) you?"

"She ______________ (lie) on the ground!", Dopey ____________ (say) and

____________ (start) to cry.

4 Finde die Fehler. Streiche die falschen Stellen durch und verbessere den Satz in den Leerzeilen. ___/10

a) Last year Mr Johnson doesn't move to Brighton.

____

b) Doesn't he have a car accident last week?

____

c) After school George goed to his aunt's house.

____

d) Peter and Susan was reading the Sunday newspaper.

____

e) Tom: "The past tense form of 'buy' is 'buyed'".

____

f) Sue: "Must I read this Book?" – Dad: "No, you mustn't."

____

g) Max are going on holiday to France next month.

____

h) Haven't she got a new bike?

____

i) This movie is very old. They make it in 1960.

____

j) Must I post the letter? – No, you mustn't.

____

Gesamtpunktzahl ____/46

4 Nomen

Nomen, auch Substantive oder Hauptwörter genannt, gehören zu den wichtigsten Bestandteilen von Sätzen. Sie können zum Beispiel als Subjekt eines Satzes, als dessen Objekt oder in genaueren Bestimmungen auftauchen.

4.1 Das Geschlecht: *Gender*

Regel

Das Geschlecht der Nomen

- Im Englischen werden **Nomen** bis auf wenige Ausnahmen **immer** als **sächlich** angesehen. Es gibt also im Gegensatz zum Deutschen keine Unterschiede bei der Schreibweise des Artikels:
  the/a *house* = ***das/ein*** *Haus*, ***the/a*** *tree* = ***der/ein*** *Baum*,
  the/a *door* = ***die/eine*** *Tür*.
- Die dann dazu passenden **Pronomen** lauten ***it*** und ***its***:
  The door is closed. → ***It*** *is closed.* (***Sie*** *ist geschlossen.)*
  The roof of the house … → ***Its*** *roof … (Das Dach des Hauses …* ***Sein*** *Dach …)*
  The top of the tree … → ***Its*** *top … (**Seine** Spitze …)*

1 Füge das richtige Nomen und Pronomen ein.

a) He can't find his ______________ (Gitarre). Is ______ behind the cupboard?

b) Your ______________ (Fahrrad) is not blue. What colour is ______?

c) Our neighbour's ______________ (Garten) is wonderful. Is ______ big?

d) Jerry's skateboard isn't new. How old is ______ ?

e) Did you see the ______________ (Film) last night? ______ was brilliant.

f) Our ______________ (Auto) is new. Do you like ______?

g) My ______________ (Federmappe) is not in my satchel.
Can you see ______?

h) Did you see the Millers? – No, ______'re on holiday.

i) Did you see the Browns? – No, ______ didn't see ______.

j) George read this ______________ (Buch). He got ______ last week.

Regel

Das Geschlecht bei Personen und Tieren

- **Personen** werden immer **nach ihrem biologischen Geschlecht** (männlich oder weiblich) **behandelt**. Danach richten sich auch die verwendeten Pronomen.
  Peter met my father in Munich last week. → ***He** met **him** in **his** house.*
  Susan told aunt Maggie the story. → ***She** told **her** the story in **her** room.*

- Bei **Tieren** wird als Pronomen ***it*** verwendet, außer man kennt das Geschlecht oder das Geschlecht kann aus dem Sinnzusammenhang abgeleitet werden.
  *Look, there is my reindeer Rudolph. **He** likes Santa Claus.*
  *Say hello to my cat Grimalda. **She**'s 14 years old.*
  Aber: *Where's the cat? **It**'s under the balcony.*

2 Finde das Pronomen, das zum Nomen passt.

a) Can you see my cat Garfield? ______ likes pasta.

b) Whose dog is that? – I don't know. ______ isn't our dog.

c) In Australia we saw a female kangaroo.

______ name was Sally. ______ was six.

d) I was watching the late night news when suddenly a big black spider ran across the room. ______ had a white cross on ______ back. My uncle's cat, Madonna, was lying on the carpet. When my sister started to scream because of the spider, ______ rushed after ______ .

e) Never trick an elephant. ______ will never forget!

f) Pinkie's cage is dirty. Must ______ tidy up ______ cage today, Mum, or can I do that tomorrow?

g) Cheeky is barking. I can hear ______ barking in the garden. He doesn't like our new neighbour.

Regel

Länder-, Städte- und Eigennamen

- **Länder** und auch **Städte** werden hin und wieder als weibliche Personen betrachtet.
  England is a wonderful country full of interesting places to see.
  → *You must visit* ***her*** *many beautiful regions.*
  Have you ever been to New York? → *No, I haven't, but I've heard about* ***her*** *fantastic skyscrapers* (*skyscraper* = Wolkenkratzer).

- Dies gilt manchmal auch für **Fahrzeuge**, immer dann, wenn eine persönliche Beziehung zum Ausdruck kommt:
  The 'Titanic' sank because she hit an iceberg. ***She*** *was one of the biggest ships in those times.*

Tipp

Um das Geschlecht von Nomen genau unterscheiden zu können, gibt es noch drei weitere Möglichkeiten:

- **besondere Endungen**, z.B. *prince/princess (Prinz/Prinzessin); waiter/waitress (Kellner/Kellnerin); duke/duchess* (Herzog/Herzogin)
- **spezielle Unterscheidungen**, z.B. *uncle/aunt (Onkel/Tante); father/mother (Vater/Mutter); bull/cow (Bulle/Kuh); king/queen (König/Königin)*
- **Zusatzpartikel**, z.B. *boyfriend/girlfriend (Freund/Freundin); tomcat/cat (Kater/Katze); male crocodile/female crocodile (männliches/weibliches Krokodil)*

3 Übersetze.

a) ein weiblicher Elefant ______________________

b) zwei Kater und eine Hündin ______________________

c) die Prinzessin und die Herzogin ______________________

d) Die Kellnerin sah den Prinzen von Wales. ______________________

e) Peter fürchtet sich vor weiblichen Spinnen. ______________________

____

f) Warst du letztes Jahr in London? – Ja, ich liebe sie (diese Stadt).

____

4.2 Singular und Plural: regelmäßige Formen

Regel

Regelmäßige Pluralformen

Die meisten Nomen bilden ihre **Pluralformen regelmäßig**. Dazu hängt man an die Singularform einfach ein **-s** an.

Beispiele: *shop* → *shops*; *table* → *tables*; *bottle* → *bottles*; *cat* → *cats*

4 Übersetze. Achte auf die Pluralform.

a) drei Männer	b) zwei Schweine
c) vier Taschen	d) fünf Regenschirme
e) zwei Autos	f) sechs Klaviere
g) zehn Bäume	h) drei Schränke
i) zwei Gärten	j) elf Fenster
k) drei Fernsehgeräte	l) fünf Freunde

Regel

Besonderheiten bei regelmäßigen Pluralformen

Einige regelmäßige Pluralformen weisen Besonderheiten auf:

a) *country* → *countries*; *berry* → *berries*; *tragedy* → tragedies;
Singular: **Endung -y nach Konsonant** → Plural: Endung ***-ies***

b) **aber**: *boy* → *boys*; *way* → ways; *play* → *plays*;
Singular: **Endung -y nach Vokal** → Plural: Endung **-s**

c) *watch* → *watches*; *kiss* → *kisses*; *boss* → *bosses*; *patch* → *patches*;
Singular: **Endung auf Zischlaut** → Plural: Endung **-es**

5 Bilde die richtige Pluralform.

a) door → ____________ b) quay → ____________

c) country → ____________ d) match → ____________

e) lodge → ____________ f) chimney → ____________

g) lorry → ____________ h) batch → ____________

i) spray → ____________ j) witch → ____________

4.3 Unregelmäßige Pluralformen

Regel

Besondere Pluralformen

+ Einige Nomen, die meistens aus dem Germanischen stammen, haben ganz besondere Pluralformen. Man muss diese Formen einfach lernen. Hierzu gehören:

man – men (Mann – Männer)	*woman – women* (Frau – Frauen)	*foot – feet* (Fuß – Füße)
tooth – teeth (Zahn – Zähne)	*mouse – mice* (Maus – Mäuse)	*child – children* (Kind – Kinder)
goose – geese (Gans – Gänse)	*ox – oxen* (Ochse – Ochsen)	*sheep – sheep* (Schaf – Schafe)

+ Nomen, welche im Singular auf *-f* oder *-fe* enden, zeigen im Plural meistens die Endung *-ves*: *knife* → *knives*; *shelf* → *shelves*; *wife* → *wives*

6 Finde die Fehler und verbessere sie.

a) five calfs ____________ b) six lorrys ____________

c) a shelve ____________ d) ten kisss ____________

e) three womans ____________ f) two mens ____________

g) a mice ____________ h) all my tooths ____________

i) three sheeps ____________ j) two childs ____________

4.4 Nomen mit ausschließlich Singularformen

Regel

Nomen mit Singularformen

Einige Nomen werden im Englischen nur im Singular verwendet. Hierzu gehören:

a) einige **abstrakte Nomen** (*abstract nouns*).
*His **information was** helpful. - Seine **Information(en) war(en)** hilfreich.*
*I like his **advice**. - Ich mag **seinen/seine Ratschlag/Ratschläge**.*
auch: *music, courage (Mut), homework, knowledge (Wissen/Kenntnisse)*

b) **Substanznomen**: Sie sind nicht zählbar und haben deshalb keine Pluralform.
*I'm so thirsty. Have you got some **water** for me?*
*She needs fresh **air**.*
*He's got brown **hair**. - Er hat braune **Haare*** (Gesamthaar, nicht Einzelhaare).

c) **Sammelbegriffe** (*collective nouns*).
*Please bring my **luggage**. → Bitte bringe mein(e) **Gepäck(stücke)**.*
Auch: *furniture = Mobiliar oder Möbel; fish = Fisch* oder *Fische*.
Im Deutschen kann man solche Nomen im Singular oder Plural darstellen.

7 Übersetze.

a) Er zeigte Mut, als er auf das Hausdach stieg.

____

____

b) Ich mag Fisch sehr gerne. Kommen diese Fische aus dem Fluss?

____

____

c) Seine Ratschläge sind immer gut.

____

d) Woher hast du diese Informationen?

____

e) Sie ist nicht blond, sie hat schwarze Haare.

____

4.5 Paarwörter: *Pair nouns*

Regel

Paarwörter

- Paarwörter bezeichnen **Dinge, die aus zwei Teilen bestehen**. Diese Nomen werden sozusagen doppelt, also im Plural gezählt. Sie dürfen nicht mit Zahlwörtern oder dem unbestimmten Artikel *a* oder *an* verbunden werden.
- Das **Verb** steht bei Paarwörtern im Englischen **im Plural**.
  Beispiele: *scissors (Schere); trousers (lange Hose); binoculars (Fernglas); shorts (kurze Hose); jeans (Jeans); glasses (Brille); scales (Waage); pyjamas (Pyjama)*

8 Setze die fehlende Form der Nomen und der Verben ein.

a) Where ______ my ________________ (Hose)? No idea, where can ______ be?

b) I must cut this sheet of paper. Do you know where the ________________ ________ (Schere)?

c) I can't find my ________________ (Brille). Where ________ they?

d) I need ________________ to weigh the letter. Where ______ ______?

e) Look, there is a very beautiful bird in the garden. Go and get our ________________ (Fernglas). Can you find ______?

f) I never wear ________________ (einen Pyjama) when I go to bed, but I wear ________________ (eine kurze Hose). I can't find ________________. ________ ________ in the washing machine?

4.6 Sammelbegriffe im Plural

Regel

Sammelbegriffe im Plural

Achtung: Einige Sammelbegriffe stehen im Englischen nur im Plural. Manchmal wird außerdem der Plural verwendet, obwohl im Deutschen der Singular gebraucht wird.

englisch	deutsch
*The **stairs are** steep!*	*Die **Treppe ist** steil!*
*Many **thanks** for your letter.*	*Vielen **Dank** für deinen Brief.*
*Your **clothes are** really hip.*	*Deine **Kleidung ist** wirklich in.*
*The **surroundings are** wonderful.*	*Die **Umgebung ist** wunderschön*
*The **goods were** of the best quality.*	*Die **Ware war** von bester Qualität.*

9 Vervollständige die Tabelle.

deutsch	englisch
a) Der Dieb stahl die Ware.	
b)	We spent our summer holiday in beautiful surroundings.
c)	The letter I received was full of thanks.
d)	She fell down the stairs.
e) Der Laden verkauft *(sell)* gerade die neue Sommerkleidung.	

Info plus

Das Nomen ***news*** steht immer im Plural. Ein Verb, das sich auf *news* bezieht, steht aber immer im Singular! *News* kann im Deutschen „die Nachrichten", aber auch „die Nachricht" bedeuten. Nicht nur unter englischen Journalisten ist der Ausspruch „*Only bad news is good news.*" sehr bekannt.

Regel

people und police

- ***People*** bedeutet *die Leute/Menschen*. Das dazugehörende **Verb steht im Plural**:
  He knew many people with financial problems. - Er kannte viele Leute mit finanziellen Problemen.
  Der Genitiv von *the people* lautet ***the people's***: *I like those people's car. - Mir gefällt das Auto dieser Leute.*
  Achtung: People im **Plural** bekommt eine völlig andere Bedeutung: *Emperor Augustus ruled over many* ***peoples***. *- Kaiser Augustus regierte über viele* ***Völker***.
- ***The police*** bedeutet die Polizei. Das dazugehörige **Verb steht immer im Plural**: *The police were there at once. - Die Polizei war sofort da.*

4.7 Mengenangaben

Regel

Mengenangaben bei Stoffen, abstrakten Nomen und Paarwörtern

Stoffe wie Milch, Zucker, Mehl, Wasser und abstrakte Nomen wie Liebe, Wissen usw. sind im Deutschen und im Englischen **nicht zählbar**. Um auszudrücken, wie viel man von dem jeweiligen Stoff meint, benötigt man **Hilfskonstruktionen**.

nicht zählbar	zählbar gemacht
sugar	*four packs of sugar - vier Packungen Zucker*
water	*three bottles of water - drei Flaschen Wasser*
bread	*two slices of bread - zwei Scheiben Brot*
information	*three pieces of information - drei Informationen*

Weitere nützliche Hilfskonstruktionen: z.B. ***a piece of*** *cake - ein Stück Kuchen;* ***a bar of*** *chocolate - eine Tafel Schokolade;* ***a cup of*** *coffee - eine Tasse Kaffee;* ***a can of*** *coke - eine Dose Cola;* ***a kilo of*** *flour - ein Kilo Mehl.*

Regel

Plural von Paarwörtern

Bei Paarwörtern müssen ebenfalls **Hilfskonstruktionen** verwendet werden:
three pairs of scissors – drei Scheren; two pairs of trousers – zwei Hosen; a pair of shorts – eine kurze Hose.

10 Trage die richtige Mengenangabe ein.

a) 	b) 
c) 	d) 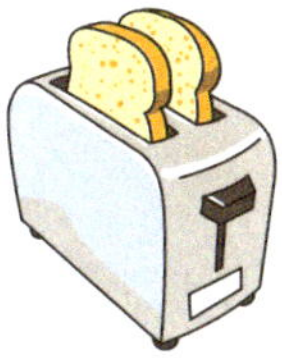
e) 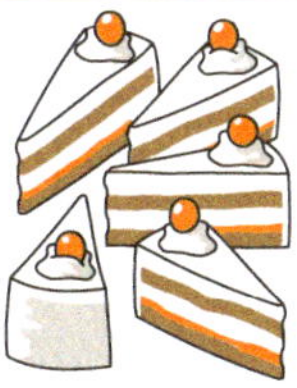	f) My advice: Take your umbrella. Don't stay too long. Take your raincoat.
g) 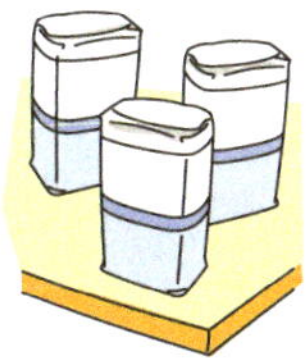	h) 
i) 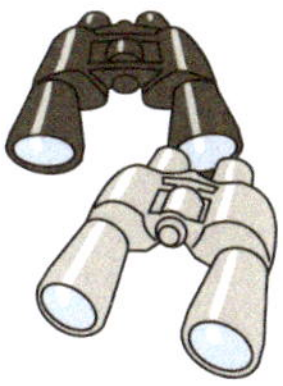	j) 

4.8 Mengenanzeiger: *Quantifiers*

Regel

much – many – some – little – few

Die folgenden Mengenanzeiger sind grundlegend wichtig. Man muss sich ihre Verwendung einprägen und dabei beachten, ob ein Nomen zählbar oder nicht zählbar ist.

Quantifier	mit zählbaren Nomen	mit nicht zählbaren Nomen
much (*viel*)	**Nicht erlaubt!**	*much air – viel Luft* *much love – viel Liebe*
many (*viele*)	*many books – viele Bücher* *many problems – viele Probleme*	**Nicht erlaubt!**
a lot of/lots of (*viele, viel*)	*a lot of houses – viele Häuser* *lots of houses – viele Häuser*	*a lot of cheese – viel Käse* *lots of sugar – viel Zucker* *a lot of help – viel Hilfe*
some (*einige/etwas*)	*some children – einige Kinder*	*some wine – etwas Wein*
a little (*wenig*)	**Nicht erlaubt!**	*a little butter – wenig Butter* *a little support – wenig Unterstützung*
few (*wenige*)	*a few cars – wenige Autos* *a few trees – wenige Bäume*	**Nicht erlaubt!**

11 Übersetze und schreibe in dein Heft.

Ein trauriger Mensch:
Ich habe nicht viel Geld, aber viele Probleme,
wenige Freunde,
einige Fragen, wenig Zeit,
etwas Geduld *(patience)* und viel Ärger *(trouble)*.

Ein glücklicher Mensch:
Ich mag viele Menschen, habe wenige Sorgen *(worries)*,
viel Geld, einige Freunde, viele Hobbys und viel Geduld.

4.9 *some* und *any*

Regel

some* und *any

- *Some* und *any* werden **bei zählbaren und nicht zählbaren Nomen** verwendet.
- ***Some*** wird grundsätzlich im **bejahten Aussagesatz** verwendet , in **bittenden Fragen** oder wenn man etwas anbieten will.
  *Can I have **some** bread? Would you like to have **some** cake?*
- ***Any*** wird im **verneinten Aussagesatz** und in **Fragen** verwendet.

a) bejahter Aussagesatz:
*There are **some** mice in the corner. – In der Ecke sind **einige** Mäuse.*
*There is **some** cheese in the fridge. – Da ist (noch) etwas Käse im Kühlschrank.*

b) verneinter Aussagesatz:
*I have**n't** got **any** problems. – Ich habe **keine** Probleme.*
*She has**n't** got **any** money left. – Sie hat **kein** Geld übrig.*

c) Fragen:
*Is there **any** time to discuss this? – Bleibt noch (**etwas**) Zeit, um dies zu besprechen?*
*Are there **any** animals in this forest? – Gibt es in diesem Wald Tiere?*

12 Füge *some* oder *any* bzw. deren Zusammensetzungen *someone, somebody* (jemand), *something* (etwas), *anyone* (irgendjemand), *anybody* (irgendjemand) oder *anything* (irgendetwas) ein.

a) Can I have ________ mustard, please. – I'm sorry, there isn't ________ left.

b) Did you here that voice? Hello, is there ________________?

c) He has ________ good ideas, but he doesn't make ________________ out of them.

d) Pete didn't say ________________ interesting at the meeting.

e) What's the matter? Is ________________ wrong? – Yes!

f) Fred needs ________________ to help him with his paper, but there isn't ________________.

g) Joe doesn't like ________ coffee. He likes tea.

h) Does ________________ know where my mother is?

4.10 Bestimmter und unbestimmter Artikel

Regel

Bestimmter und unbestimmter Artikel

- Der **bestimmte Artikel** (deutsch: der/die/das) lautet im Englischen ***the***, der **unbestimmte** (deutsch: ein/eine/ein) lautet ***a*** oder ***an***.
- Im Englischen gibt es keine Unterscheidung zwischen männlichen, weiblichen und sächlichen Nomen, deshalb muss die Unterscheidung der Geschlechter bei den Artikeln nicht beachtet werden:
  the *house;* ***the*** *ball;* ***the*** *landscape;* ***the*** *orange shirt –* ***das*** *Haus;* ***der*** *Ball;* ***die*** *Landschaft;* ***das*** *orangefarbene Hemd.*

Beim unbestimmten Artikel verwendet man zwei Formen:

a) ***a*** immer dann, wenn das darauffolgende Wort mit einem konsonantischen Laut beginnt: ***a*** *bed – ein Bett;* ***a*** *letter – ein Brief;* ***a*** *mother – eine Mutter.*

b) ***an*** immer dann, wenn das darauffolgende Wort mit einem vokalischen Laut beginnt: ***an*** *orange;* ***an*** *old car;* ***an*** *eagle;* ***an*** *interesting book;* ***an*** *armchair.*

13 Finde den richtigen unbestimmten Artikel.

In my satchel I have got ______ pencil, ______ orange pen, ______ old book, ______ photo of my dog, ______ beautiful pencil case, ______ extra ruler and ________ used model car (!).

4.11 Groß- und Kleinschreibung von Nomen

Regel

Groß- und Kleinschreibung

Nomen werden im Englischen im Gegensatz zum Deutschen **grundsätzlich klein** geschrieben. Allerdings gibt es hierbei zwei Ausnahmen:

a) Nomen stehen am **Satzanfang** (dann Großschreibung): ***Tigers*** *are dangerous animals.* Aber: *The* ***tiger*** *is a dangerous animal.*

b) Es handelt sich um Eigennamen oder geographische Bezeichnungen (dann Großschreibung): *I met* ***Mum*** *in the bus.* (aber: *I met my* ***mum*** *in the bus.*) *I was born in* ***Germany****. She saw* ***Mr Miller*** *in the garden. The* ***UN*** *(****United Nations****) help a lot of poor countries. We went into* ***Oxford Street****.*

Achtung: bei **Orts-, Länder-, Völker- und Kontinentbezeichnungen** werden nicht nur die Nomen, sondern auch die zugehörigen **Adjektive großgeschrieben**:
Great Britain - British, England - English, Ireland - Irish, Scotland - Scottish, Wales - Welsh, Italy - Italian, Switzerland - Swiss, Austria - Austrian, Spain - Spanish, Russia - Russian, Rome - Roman, America - American, Asia - Asian, Africa - African, Australia - Australian, Bavaria - Bavarian.

14 Arbeite mithilfe eines Wörterbuches und ergänze die Tabelle.

deutsch	englisch
a) ein norwegischer Fischer	
b) irische Schafe	
c) Hunde aus England	
d) ein schottischer Dudelsack *(bagpipe)*	
e) die Straßen in Wales	
f) Mein Onkel heißt Tom.	
g) Ich mag Tante Margaret.	
h) Unser Haus ist in der Königsstraße.	
i) Papa, kannst du mich sehen?	

Tipp

Im Internet gibt es verschiedene freie **Online-Lexika**, z.B. LEO mit einem englisch-deutschen Wörterbuch unter www.leo.org.

Info plus

Der **Dudelsack *(bagpipe)*** stammt übrigens nicht ursprünglich aus Schottland. Schon im antiken Griechenland war dieses Instrument bekannt, aber auch in Indien, China und im antiken Rom. Vermutlich kam der Dudelsack im Laufe der Eroberungszüge Caesars im 1. Jahrhundert v. Chr. nach England und von dort zu den Schotten. Viele Jahrhunderte lang galt der Dudelsack als Kriegsinstrument, wurde im 16. und 18. Jahrhundert daher sogar zweimal verboten.
Heute hat er seinen kriegerischen Charakter verloren und gilt in der ganzen Welt als schottisches Nationalinstrument.

33 Wie lauten die Personalpronomen zu englischen Nomen, wenn es sich nicht um Personen handelt?

34 Welche Nomengruppen können grammatikalisch als weiblich bezeichnet werden?

35 Wie wird der regelmäßige Plural eines englischen Nomens gebildet?

36 Welche beiden Pluralregelungen gibt es für Nomen, die im Singular auf *-y* enden? Nenne zwei Beispiele.

37 Wie bildet man den Plural von *information*?

38 Worin besteht der Unterschied zwischen *little* und *few*?

39 Wann verwendet man *some*, wann *any*?

40 Welche Nomen und welche Adjektive werden immer großgeschrieben?

1 Schreibe das richtige Pronomen hinter den durchgestrichenen Teil. ___/14

a) ~~My father~~ ______ repaired ~~our car Jenny~~ ______ yesterday. But today ~~the car~~ ______ broke down again. I hope ~~my dad and I~~ ______ will have ~~Jenny~~ ______ back soon.

b) Did you see ~~the new teacher~~ ______ in ~~the gym~~ ______? – No, I didn't, but I saw ~~Mrs Box~~ ______. She was holding ~~a tomcat~~ ______ in ~~her arms~~ ______.

c) ~~Tanja's~~ ______ shoes are not blue, ~~her shoes~~ ______'re green and orange.

d) Great Britain is a nice place to spend a holiday. ~~Great Britain~~ ______ is fantastic.

e) Why did the 'Titanic' sink? – ~~The 'Titanic'~~ ______ sank because she hit an iceberg.

2 Erstelle eine Einkaufsliste. ___/14

Drei Dosen Katzenfutter *(cat fodder)* für meinen Kater Tom, zwei Scheren, ein Kilo Zucker, zwei Messer, vier Tassen, fünf Riegel Schokolade, zwei Hefte für den Sohn unseres Nachbarn, drei Armbanduhren (Singular: *wrist watch*) für die Kinder meiner Tante, etwas Salbe *(ointment)* für die Füße meiner Oma und drei Schachteln Zündhölzer *(matches)*.

I must buy ____

__/9

3 Übersetze.

Letzte Nacht träumte ich von *(to dream of)* drei Männern und zwei Frauen. Sie hatten große Füße und wenige Zähne. Sie sprachen mit vier Kindern und spielten mit sechs Mäusen, zwei Gänsen, vier Ochsen und fünf Schafen.

__/5

4 Streiche die jeweils falsche Form durch.

a) I didn't get his information/informations. It/They was/were not very helpful.
b) At the beginning he was rather bad at Mathematic/Mathematics. But in the course of the year he improved his knowledge/knowledges.
c) Has she got brown eye/eyes and red hair/hairs?
d) Would you please take my pieces of luggage/luggages to the station?
e) Your living room's got nice furniture/furnitures.

__/6

5 Bringe die folgende Redeabsicht ins Englische.

Du teilst jemandem mit, dass du für ihn eine gute Nachricht hast. Du sagst ihm, dass er seinen Winterurlaub in einer wunderbaren Umgebung in Österreich verbringen kann. Du rätst ihm, lange Hosen und ein Fernglas mitzunehmen.

6 Setze *some* und *any* und die richtigen Mengenanzeiger *(quantifiers)* wie *few, little* oder *many* ein. ___/10

a) ________ people have a bike, but ________ people have a helicopter.

b) Have you got ________ time for me this weekend? – No, I haven't ________ .

c) Have you got 20 euros? – No, I've only got 1 euro. – Oh, that's only a ________ money.

d) In Germany there are ________ people with no jobs at the moment. –

Oh yes, that is really a big problem in __________ parts of the country.

e) Is there ____________ I must know? – No, there aren't ________ problems.

f) There is _______________ to say about this man. He's mad.

7 Setze den richtigen Artikel *the/a/an* und den richtigen Buchstaben in die Lücke ein. Achte dabei auf Groß- und Kleinschreibung. ___/32

a) _____ lion is a very dangerous animal from ___frica. This animal lives in the

central ___frican plains (= Ebenen). It's got _____ orange fur (= Fell).

b) I bought _____ three watches in _____ ___wiss shop.

c) I like _____ ___erman football team very much. – No, I think _____ ___nglish

team is better. – But _____ best team is _____ team from ___rasil.

d) I need _____ new pen, _____ orange pencil case, three _____ pens, my new

T-shirt from ___taly and my ___panish book.

e) Listen, do you want to tell me _____ old story? I heard about this boy

from ___rance yesterday. My sister told me _____ story.

f) ___avaria is a part of ___ermany and ___urope.

g) _____ apple _____ day keeps _____ doctor away.

h) _____ tiger is _____ ___frican or ___ndian animal.

Gesamtpunktzahl ____/90

5 Adjektive, Adverbien und adverbiale Bestimmungen

Adjektive und Adverbien haben im Deutschen meist die gleiche Form. Deshalb müssen wir Deutschen meist gar nicht darüber nachdenken, ob wir nun ein Adjektiv oder ein Adverb verwenden. Ganz anders ist es im Englischen: Dort gibt es für das Adjektiv und Adverb jeweils unterschiedliche Formen – mit Ausnahmen. Wer die richtige Form verwenden will, muss verstehen, welche unterschiedlichen Aufgaben Adjektiv und Adverb im Satz haben.

5.1 Adjektive und Adverbien

Regel

Adjektive

Adjektive *(adjectives)* geben Auskunft darüber, **wie etwas ist**. Sie beschreiben Nomen, d.h. Namenwörter, genauer.
Adjektive stehen **vor dem Nomen**: *the nice boy, the fast car, the green bike.*
Adjektive stehen auch im Zusammenhang mit dem Verb *be*: *The boy is nice.*

1 On holiday on a campsite

Setze die Adjektive richtig ein:
excited – many – bad – sad (2x) – muddy (matschig) – happy (2x) – a lot of – exciting – dirty – big – small – fine

__________ people spend their holidays on campsites. They live in __________ caravans and are __________ when the weather is __________. When the weather is __________, they aren't so __________. Then you can see them walk around with __________ faces and __________ umbrellas. But not all people are __________. Children often have __________ fun in the rain. They try to hop across __________ puddles or are __________ when they can walk through them. Their mothers often do not think that this is __________, because they have to wash the __________ clothes.

Tipp

much, many und a lot of

much verwendet man für nicht zählbare Nomen: *much coffee, much love*.
many muss man für zählbare Nomen verwenden: *many people, many trees*.
a lot of wird für zählbare und nicht zählbare Nomen verwendet: *a lot of bottles, a lot of fun*

Regel

Adverbien und adverbiale Bestimmungen

Adverbien und adverbiale Bestimmungen (dt.: Umstandswörter, Adverbiale; engl.: *adverbs, adverbials*) zeigen an, wie oder wie oft, wo oder zu welcher Zeit man etwas tut. Sie **beschreiben Verben, Adjektive, andere Adverbien** und sogar ganze **Sätze** näher.
Es gibt zum Beispiel **Häufigkeitsadverbien** *(adverbs of frequency)* oder **Zeit- und Ortsadverbien** *(adverbs und adverbials of time and place)*.

2 Unterstreiche die Adverbien.

a) My friend Bob always spends his holidays on a campsite in France.

b) His parents never want to spend their holidays in a hotel.

c) Sometimes I can go with Bob and his parents.

d) Bob and I always have a lot of fun in our tent.

5.2 Häufigkeitsadverbien

Regel

Häufigkeitsadverbien

- Wie der Name schon sagt, geben **Häufigkeitsadverbien** *(adverbs of frequency)* Auskunft darüber, ob eine Handlung oft, manchmal, immer, regelmäßig, normalerweise, selten oder nie stattfindet *(often, sometimes, always, regularly, normally, rarely, never)*.
- Diese Adverbien stehen im Englischen im Unterschied zum Deutschen **direkt vor dem Vollverb**.
  He always goes to school at eight in the morning.
- Wenn sich die Adverbien auf das Verb *to be* beziehen und ein Adjektiv oder direktes Objekt folgt, stehen sie **nach den Formen von *be***.
  He is never late. He is always a gentleman.

3 Schreibe auf, was Sandy wie oft tut. Verwende die Adverbien: *always, never, sometimes, often*.

	Monday	Tuesday	Wednesday	Thursday	Friday	Saturday	Sunday
 pl.			X			X	
 pl.							
	X	X	X	X	X	X	X
			X		X	X	X

Sandy ____.

Sandy ____.

Sandy ____.

Sandy ____.

5.3 Adverbiale Bestimmungen von Zeit und Ort

Regel

Achtung bei der Satzstellung!

- **Zeitadverbien und -adverbiale** sind zum Beispiel: *yesterday, last week, today, last year, ten years ago, in 1988, on Monday(s)*, aber auch Zusammensetzungen mit ***every***: *every week/day/morning/year* usw.
- **Ortsadverbien und -adverbiale** sind zum Beispiel: *here, there, at school, in the park, in front of the house, under the car, behind the curtain* usw.
- Bei diesen Adverbien muss man sich die Satzstellung einprägen. Grundsätzlich gilt bei Zeit- und Ortsangaben:
  Ort vor Zeit! **Richtung vor Ort!**
  Genaues vor Allgemeines! *(z.B. Uhrzeit vor Tag, Straße vor Stadtviertel)*
- Das **Adverb** steht **nie zwischen Verb und Objekt!**

4 Bilde Sätze. Finde die richtige Satzstellung.

a) he - every morning - in High Street - breakfast - at a café - has

____.

b) they - to Britain - are going to - tomorrow - go

____.

c) he - at 7.30 - his house - every day - leaves

____.

d) he - rode - every Sunday afternoon - through the forest - his bike

____.

e) in Hatfield - goes - to her grandmother - Sandra - every weekend

____.

f) played - the guitar - last year - he - in Broad Street - every Saturday - at a club

____

5 Die Wörter in diesen Sätze sind durcheinandergeraten. Verbessere die Sätze.

a) He was born in 1988 in London on the 11th of April.

____.

b) I saw a film star this morning at the station.

____.

c) She lost her dog last Tuesday in the underground in the morning.

____

____.

d) She went last week in Broad Street every afternoon to the supermarket.

____

____.

e) She bought there a pound of butter always.

____.

Tipp

Gibt es mehrere Zeit- und Ortsadverbien bzw. -adverbiale in einem Satz, so kann man vor allem Zeitadverbien und -adverbiale auch an den Anfang des Satzes stellen.
Beispiel: *Every weekend in summer Sandra goes to her grandmother in Hatfield.*
Man vermeidet so eine Anhäufung von Adverbien am Satzende und kann flüssigere Sätze bilden.

6 Bringe die Wörter in die richtige Reihenfolge und vermeide dabei „Adverbienhäufchen" am Satzende.

a) played the guitar - last year - he - in Broad Street - every Saturday - at a club

____.

b) was with him - his girlfriend - every night - next to the stage *(= Bühne)* - at a table

____

____.

c) never - looked - from the stage - he - at her - all evening

____.

d) always - the young lady - the newspaper - in the morning - reads - at breakfast - in the diningroom - on Sundays ______________________

____.

e) at the weekend - read - in my room - I - the new Harry Potter - on the sofa - all day long.

____

____

f) Make your special "super-adverbial-sentence".

____

____

Tipp

Adverbien in der richtigen Reihenfolge

- Um sich die richtige Reihenfolge der Adverbien zu merken, muss man sich eigentlich nur die Reihenfolge der Anfangsbuchstaben der Satzglieder merken: Subjekt - Prädikat (Verb) - Objekt S - P(V) - O
  + Häufigkeit **H**
  + Ort **O**
  + Zeit **Z**
  Die Reihenfolge heißt dann:
  S - **H** - P - O - **O - Z**
- Trick: Du kannst aus den Anfangsbuchstaben auch ein fiktives Wort bilden. Es würde in diesem Falle wohl „Schpuus" ausgesprochen.
- Eine zusätzliche Möglichkeit, dir die Reihenfolge der Adverbien einzuprägen, ist es, einen möglichst komischen oder lustigen Satz zu bilden und sich diesen zu merken, z. B.: *Mister Miller never picks his nose at school on Fridays.*
  Subjekt - H - P/V - Objekt - Ort - Zeit

(*to pick one's nose* = in der Nase bohren)

7 Trage die Adverbien, adverbialen Bestimmungen und Adjektive in die Tabelle ein.

in the morning - funny - normally - at school - before Christmas - sweet - always - next to Sandra - after the holidays - strong - at night - at my neighbour's house - never - sad - every Monday night - nice - in bed - happy - at home - in summer

Adverb der Häufigkeit	Ortsangabe	Zeitangabe	Adjektiv

41 Worauf beziehen sich Adjektive? ______________________

42 Worauf können sich Adverbien beziehen? ______________________

____

43 An welcher Stelle darf in englischen Aussagesätzen nie ein Adverb stehen? Trage das Adverb an der richtigen Stelle ein.

S ______________ P(V) ______________ O

44 Wie nennt man die Adverbien der Häufigkeit im Englischen?

____

45 - **51** Trage die Adverbien bzw. adverbialen Bestimmungen ein.

englisch	deutsch
45	immer
46 sometimes	
47	um 8.30 Uhr
48	oft
49 never	
50	zuhause
51 in the evening	

52 Für welche Nomen verwendet man *much*? Notiere ein Beispiel.

____

53 Für welche Nomen verwendet man *many*? Notiere ein Beispiel.

____

54 Welche Satzstellung muss bei Adverbien der Zeit, des Ortes und der Richtung eingehalten werde? ______________________

1 Unterstreiche die Satzglieder:
Subjekt (blau), Prädikat/Verb (grün), Objekt (gelb), die Adverbien der Zeit (orange), des Ortes (braun) und die der Häufigkeit (violett). ___/3

Mr Miller never picks his nose at school in the morning.

2 Übersetze den Text. ___/42

Mike war gestern im Kino. Er saß in Reihe *(row)* drei. Zuerst sah er alles, aber dann setzten sich eine Frau und ein Mann vor ihn. Mike sagte zu der Frau: „Ich gehe (sonst) nie ins Kino. Heute bin ich hier und ich will diesen Film sehen. Suchen Sie sich bitte neue Sitzplätze." (suchen = *look for*; Sitzplätze = *seats*). Die Frau antwortete: „Das tut mir leid. Mein Mann und ich kommen jeden Sonntag um 18 Uhr hierher (Ehemann = *husband*). Wir sitzen immer hier." Dann kam ein dicker Mann ins Kino. Er kannte die Frau. Er sagte: „Hallo, Margarete, du bist auch hier? Ich kaufe normalerweise im Kinoladen *(shop)* Popcorn. Heute aber habe ich eine Freikarte *(free ticket)* und ich vergaß mein Geld zuhause. Bitte bezahle heute meine Popcorn."

__/12 **3** *Time for friends?* Bilde Sätze und beschreibe wo, wie oft und wann Sandra ihren Wochenplan erfüllt.

It's Easter and there are holidays. But Sandra has got a lot to do. She had bad marks in Maths (so her mother won't let her go out in the evenings) and is preparing for a piano concert. And Sandra doesn't want to stop her other activities.

Monday	Tuesday	Wednesday	Thursday	Friday	Saturday	Sunday
morning: practise the piano	morning: piano lesson (school)	morning: revise Maths, practise the piano	morning: practise the piano	morning: piano lesson (school)	morning: sleep long, read	morning: practise the piano
afternoon: revise Maths!	afternoon: practise the piano, drama group	afternoon: football	afternoon: ballet lesson	afternoon: football	afternoon: practise the piano	after-noon: sleep
			evening: Movie Club	evening: practise the piano		evening: THE CONCERT

a) (piano lessons) ____________________

____

b) (practise the piano) ____________________

____

c) (repeat Maths) ____________________

____

d) (Movie Club) ____________________

____

e) (football) ____________________

____

f) Time for friends? ____________________

4 Finde aus der Wortschlange Adverbien, adverbiale Bestimmungen und Adjektive heraus und trage sie in die richtige Spalte der Tabelle ein. ___/19

angryneversadlonelyatschoolinthemorninghappyalwaysintheafternoonyes terdayatthesupermarketsometimesatnightinthecityeveryWednesdayfun nyniceinmyholidaysinEngland

Adjektiv	Adverb der Häufigkeit	Adverbiale der Zeit	Adverbiale des Ortes

5 Bringe die Worte in die richtige Reihenfolge. Ergänze die Satzzeichen. ___/5

a) Mike - gets up - at seven - normally

____.

b) Sometimes - can - he - sleep late - in the morning

____.

c) Always - Mike - to school by bike - goes

____.

d) His father - gives him a lift - never - on Saturday - in the morning

____

____.

e) Says - always - his father - "there's no bad weather, only the wrong clothes!"

____.

Gesamtpunktzahl ___/81

6 Präpositionen

Präpositionen sind Verhältniswörter. Durch sie erkennen wir zum Beispiel eine Orts-, Richtungs- oder Zeitbeziehung. Präpositionen des Ortes, der Richtung und der Zeit sind wichtige Satzelemente. Schließlich ist es nicht ganz unwichtig, ob sich eine Maus vor, neben oder in der Speisekammer befindet.

6.1 Präpositionen des Ortes: *Prepositions of Place*

Regel

Wichtige Präpositionen des Ortes

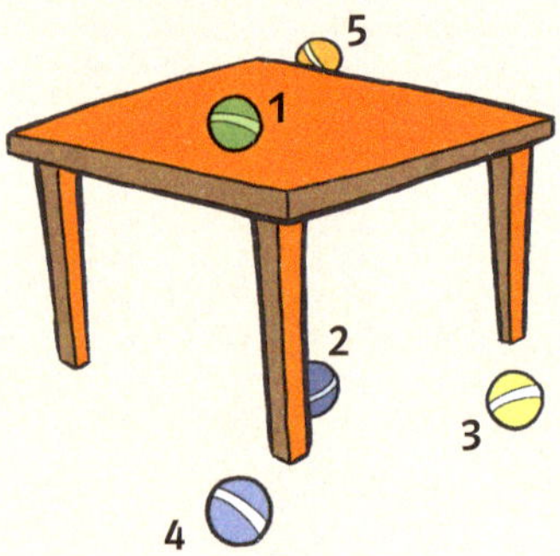

1 *The ball is **on** the table.*

2 *The ball is **under** the table.*

3 *The ball is **next to** the table.*

4 *The ball is **in front of** the table.*

5 *The ball is **behind** the table.*

1 Bilde Sätze.

a) The lion is ____________________

b) The dog is ____________________

c) The giraffe is ____________________

d) The kangaroo is ____________________

e) The birds are ____________________

f) The trees are ____________________

g) The boy is ____________________

Regel

in, at, below, under, between, among, opposite **und** ***above***

Bei diesen Präpositionen muss man besonders aufpassen:

- ***In*** bezieht sich in der Regel auf einen **abgeschlossenen Raum**.
  in the room, in my pencil-case, in our church
  Aber: *in the street - auf der Straße; in the country - auf dem Land*
- ***At*** bezieht sich auf die **Einrichtung/Institution**.
  at school - in der Schule; at work - bei der Arbeit; at the doctor's - beim Arzt
- ***Below*** bedeutet eher **unterhalb**, ***under*** bedeutet **unter**.
  The hole is below the window. - Das Loch ist unterhalb des Fensters.
  The book is under the bed. - Das Buch ist (liegt) unter dem Bett.
- ***Between*** bedeutet immer räumlich **zwischen zwei Bezugspunkten**.
  Mary is standing between Peter and Paul.
- ***Among*** bedeutet „unter Menschen" im Sinne von „in einer Gruppe".
  Among the pupils there are two people with glasses. - Unter den Schülern sind zwei mit Brille.
- ***Opposite*** bedeutet **gegenüber.**
  The town hall is opposite the station. - Das Rathaus befindet sich gegenüber des Bahnhofs.
- ***Above*** bedeutet **darüber** oder **über hinweg**.
  A stork is flying above the church. - Ein Storch fliegt gerade über die Kirche (hinweg).

2 Unterstreiche zuerst die Ortspräposition und übersetze dann.

a) Das Haus der Johnsons liegt zwischen der Sporthalle *(gym)* und der Kirche.

____

b) Gegenüber des Brunnens *(fountain)* ist ein alter Baum.

____

c) Jenny hat eine Narbe *(scar)* unterhalb des Ellenbogens *(elbow)*.

____

d) Unter den Schülern befinden sich fünf Engländer.

____

e) Auf dem Land gibt es viel frische Luft.

f) Susan ist nicht hier, sie ist in der Schule.

g) Wo ist mein Handy *(mobile phone)*? – Es liegt (ist) unter dem Stuhl.

h) In New York kannst du viele gelbe Taxis *(taxis)* auf den Straßen sehen.

i) Mein Vater fliegt heute nach Boston. Er fliegt gerade über Grönland *(Greenland)* hinweg.

3 Vergleiche den Text mit dem Bild, unterstreiche die Ortspräpositionen und ordne sie dann den deutschen Entsprechungen in der Tabelle auf der nächsten Seite zu.

Mr Smith is standing in front of his house. Bianca, his daughter, is in the house. There is a tree behind the house. Paul is lying under it. Mrs Smith is at the supermarket. She's in the building. Grandpa and Grandma are sitting opposite each other on the first floor. There's a table between them. Bianca is on the floor below. The cat is on the roof. A helicopter is flying above the house. There are six people between the supermarket and the Smiths' house. Among them are two women and one girl.

im		hinter	
vor		unter	
zwischen		gegenüber	
über (hinweg)		auf	
unterhalb		darunter	

4 Beschreibe, was die Tiere und Personen gerade tun.

a)

b)

c)

d)

e)

a) The cat is ____________ ________ the chair.

b) Sarah is ________ ___ school. She's ________ ___ a desk.

c) Laura is ________ ______ ___ Stan.

d) The dog is ____________ ________ the bush.

e) Tim is ____________ ________ the students.

6.2 Richtungspräpositionen: *Prepositions of Direction*

Regel

Richtungspräpositionen: Verwendung und Formen

Richtungspräpositionen verraten etwas über eine **Richtung** oder eine **Bewegung**, also ob sich zum Beispiel etwas nach oben, nach unten, in etwas hinein oder aus etwas heraus bewegt.

Wichtige Präpositionen sind:

up	hinauf/herauf	*across*	über/quer über
down	hinunter/herunter	*around*	um/um herum
to	zu/in Richtung	*through*	durch (hindurch)
into	hinein	*over*	über/quer über
out (of)	hinaus/heraus	*past*	an/am … vorbei
from	von (weg)	*right/left*	(nach) rechts/links

5 Schreibe die englischen Präpositionen in die Tabelle.

a) 	a)
b) 	b)
c) 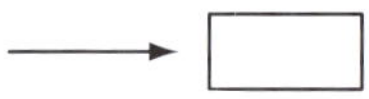	c)
d) 	d)
e) 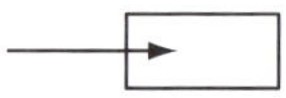	e)
f) 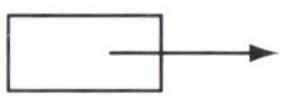	f)
g) 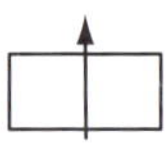	g)
h) 	h)

Tipp

in und *into*

Verwechsle nie ***in*** und ***into***. *In* ist eine reine Ortspräposition, *into* (in etwas hinein) ist eine Richtungspräposition!

Achtung: Im Deutschen werden oft Unterschiede gemacht, wo im Englischen die gleichen Präpositionen stehen.

*Sie gehen gerade ins Schloss **hinein**.* → *They are going **into** the castle.*
*Sie kommen gerade in den Raum **herein**.* → *They are coming **into** the room.*
*Er geht gerade (die Treppe) **hinunter**.* → *He is going **downstairs**.*
*Er kommt gerade (die Treppe) **herunter**.* → *He is coming **downstairs**.*
*Sie geht gerade (die Treppe) **hinauf**.* → *She is going **upstairs**.*
*Sie kommt gerade (die Treppe) **herauf**.* → *She is coming **upstairs**.*
*Du gehst gerade den Berg **hinauf**.* → *You are going **up** the hill.*
*Du kommst gerade den Berg **herauf**.* → *You are coming **up** the hill.*

6 Übersetze.

a) … in den Zoo *(zoo)* hinein …	b) … aus der Schachtel *(box)* heraus …	c) … am See *(lake)* vorbei …
d) … um den Turm *(tower)* herum …	e) … über die Straße …	f) … durch den Garten hindurch …
g) … auf dem Gipfel *(summit)* …	h) … zum Rathaus *(town hall)* …	i) … vom Zaun *(fence)* her …
j) … die Treppe herauf …	k) … an mir vorbei …	e) … die Leiter *(ladder)* hinunter …

7 Schau dir die Zeichnung an und schließe die Lücken.

If you want to go ________________ the hill, you go along the river *(Fluss)*. You walk ________________ the big tree and go ________________ the bridge.

________________ the bridge there is a forest *(Wald)*. At the end of the forest, there is a big rock *(Felsen)*. There are usually people standing ________________ top of it. You walk ________________ the rock and then you go ________________ for some time and go ________________ for a few minutes and reach a small pond *(Teich)*. ________________ the pond you can see the witch's cottage *(Hexenhaus)*. You walk ________________ the witch's cottage.

________________ top of the hill there is a cross *(Kreuz)*. Then you can see the lake *(See)* ________________ in the plain *(Ebene)*. Very often big birds fly ________________ it.

6.3 Zeitpräpositionen: *Prepositions of Time*

Regel

Zeitpräpositionen: Funktion und Formen

Zeitpräpositionen geben an, zu welchem Zeitpunkt oder in welchem Zeitraum etwas geschieht.

dt.	engl.	Erklärung	Beispiel
vor	***ago***	Wird nachgestellt und bestimmt eine Zeit in der Vergangenheit.	*Ten minutes ago …* *2000 years ago …*
	before	Steht vor dem Zeitpunkt/Zeitraum der Vergangenheit, auf welchen es sich bezieht.	*Before 1988 …* *Before the war …*
	to	bei Uhrzeiten	*Ten to six …*
nach	***past***	bei Uhrzeiten	*Ten past six …*
	after	bei Tageszeiten, Geschehnissen	*After dinner …* *After the goldrush (nach dem Goldrausch) …*
am	***on***	für Wochentage	*On Monday*
	in	bei Tageszeiten	*In the evening/morning/afternoon …*
	at	Wochenende, Feiertage	*At the weekend ...* *At Easter (an Ostern) …*
in/im	***at***	nachts	*At night …*
	in	bei Monaten und Jahresangaben	*In April …* *In 2525 (im Jahr 2525) …*
um	***at***	bei Uhrzeiten	*At six o'clock …*
bis	***until/till***	für eine Zeitdauer	*Till Monday …/Until Monday*
	by	bis zu einem Zeitpunkt	*He'll come by six. (Er wird bis spätestens sechs Uhr kommen.)*
während	***during***	bei Zeiträumen	*During lunchbreak …*

8 Fülle jede Lücke.

a) In English speaking countries, children don´t get their presents __________ Christmas Eve (December 24th). They have to wait __________ Christmas Day (December 25th).

b) __________ Christmas Eve people usually go to church __________ the evening.

c) __________ church, children hang a Christmas stocking *(Strumpf)* close to the fireplace. __________ night Father Christmas comes through the chimney *(Schornstein)* of the house and brings the presents. So __________ the children go to bed, they are usually very excited.

d) __________ the morning of Christmas Day, children usually get up very early to unwrap *(auspacken)* their presents. Many children already get up __________ six o´clock!

e) __________ the afternoon, Christmas dinner is served.

f) By the way: about hundred and sixty years __________ people in Britain decorated the first Christmas trees.

Info plus

Boxing Day

Der zweite Weihnachtstag wird in England und in anderen Ländern des Commonwealth *Boxing Day* genannt. Dieser Name wird heute auf unterschiedliche Gegebenheiten zurückgeführt. So sollen beispielsweise am *Boxing Day* den Hausangestellten britischer Adliger Geschenke in Schachteln *(boxes)* überreicht worden sein. Eine andere Quelle besagt, dass an Weihnachten in den Kirchen in einer Schachtel Geld für die Armen gesammelt wurde. Außerdem war es in Großbritannien üblich, dass die Angestellten nach dem Weihnachtsfest zu ihren Herren gingen, um sich dort in einer Schachtel einen Jahresbonus, also eine Art Weihnachtsgeld, abzuholen.

Tipp

Präpositionen bestimmen beispielsweise Beziehungen zu Orts-, Zeit- und Richtungsangaben. Verwechsle sie nicht mit Bindewörtern, den ***Konjunktionen***. Diese verbinden Satzteile, Nebensätze und Hauptsätze miteinander.

Wichtige Konjunktionen sind zum Beispiel: *and* (und), *because* (weil). Aber auch *after* (nachdem) und *before* (bevor) sind Konjunktionen. Diese Wörter hast du bisher als Präpositionen kennengelernt.

9 Setze die richtigen Präpositionen und Konjunktionen ein.

a) I met her ________ school ________ I asked her a lot of questions ________ she is very intelligent.

b) When I was ________ top of the hill, I had a wonderful view ________ the valley ________ I was absolutely happy.

c) ________ she had breakfast, she brushed her teeth ________ the bathroom.

d) Put the ruler ________ the table please, ________ then fix the new poster ________ the wall.

e) I didn't find out what was happening, ________ Sue and Pete didn't tell me about it.

10 Versuche, das Gedicht der Präpositionen zu lernen.

A poem of prepositions

Up *and* ***down*** *the hill,*
into *and* ***out of*** *the mill,*
past *and* ***around*** *our school,*
to *and* ***from*** *the pool,*
across *or* ***over*** *the bridge,*
through *the house of the witch.*

Trotz schlechter Dichtung,
zeigen diese Präpositionen die Richtung!

55 Welche drei Arten von Präpositionen kennst du jetzt?

______

56 – 61 Gib die englischen Präpositionen an und übersetze.

56 auf dem Dach ______

57 unter dem Heft ______

58 neben der Tür ______

59 hinter dir ______

60 vor dem Baum ______

61 über das Haus hinweg ______

62 – 66 Nenne die jeweiligen gegensätzlichen Präpositionen.

62 up → ______

63 out of → ______

64 to → ______

65 downstairs → ______

66 in front of → ______

67 Erkläre den wesentlichen Unterschied zwischen ***in*** und ***into***.

in: ______

into: ______

68 Welchen Überbegriff gibt es für Wörter wie ***because*** und ***and.***

______

69 Wie kann die Präposition *vor* ins Englische übersetzt werden? Erkläre die jeweilige Bedeutung.

______

______

______

1 Setze passende Präpositionen ein. ___/20

Mr Jorgensen is __________ a conference. Suddenly his boss looks __________ him. "Have you got your folder *(Aktenordner, Mappe)* with you?" he asks. Mr Jorgensen looks everywhere: __________ his bag and __________ the desk. He can't find it. "I'm sure I put it __________ my bag this morning, but it's not there. It must be __________ home. I can call my wife __________ the telephone!" he says. He goes __________ the phone. The phone is __________ him __________ the window. "Hello! Oh, sweet baby, can I talk __________ Mummy, please?" Mr Jorgensen says __________ his daughter. His boss looks __________ him strangely. "Hello, darling, I forgot my folder. Can you please look __________ my desk. … Oh, it isn't there. Then it must be __________ the bedside table __________ our bedroom. … No? Then it can only be __________ the newspaper __________ the breakfast table. No? What? You threw the newspaper __________ the dustbin *(Mülleimer, Mülltonne)* this morning! Bye, see you later __________ the party."

2 *in* oder *into*? Setze ein. ___/11

Mrs Miller is __________ the bank __________ Salisbury at the moment. Klaus is going __________ the bank. His money is __________ his pocket. Mrs Miller is putting all her money __________ her bag when Klaus sees a gangster coming __________ the building. He's got a gun __________ his hand! He waits for a moment __________ the building, then takes all the money, runs out and turns __________ Main Street. Thank God, the people __________ the bank are not __________ danger any longer.

__/37,5 **3** Lies den Text. Unterstreiche die Präpositionen grün und die Konjunktionen blau. Übersetze den Text anschließend und schreibe ihn in dein Heft.

One Friday evening Andy and David had a funny adventure in the garden. After lunch they put up a tent, because they wanted to sleep in it. They put their sleeping bags and their torches into the tent and waited for the night to come. "We could go to bed while the news is on", Andy said. "No, let's wait until it is dark.", David answered. But it was summer and there was a nice film on TV, and they couldn't go out so fast, because they were playing 'Snakes and Ladders' with Bianca and Tammy. When they finally wanted to go to bed it was raining cats and dogs and Mrs Smith said, "You can't sleep in the garden tonight. You will get wet in the tent!"

__/20 **4** Andys Katze, Bonkers, ist ein sehr lebhaftes Tier. Fülle die Lücken aus.

Bonkers likes cars, so she is ______________ *(im)* the car very often. Sometimes, when it rains, she sleeps ______________ *(unter)* the car, and when the sun shines, Bonkers likes to be ______________ *(auf)* the car roof. After her nap (Mittagsschlaf) she jumps ______________ *(vom)* the car and stretches her legs ______________ *(davor)* it. Then she usually walks ______________ *(zur)* the other side of the car and wants to sleep again. But what's this? There are four dogs ______________ *(im)* the garden. They are ______________ *(neben)* the garden shed. Suddenly she is a cat alone ______________ *(mit/unter)* four dogs! She jumps ______________ *(hinunter)* the car and runs ______________ *(zum)* the tree. She climbs ______________ *(hinauf)*. Now, she's a cat ______________ *(auf)* the tree! But she can't go ______________ *(herunter)* again, because one of the four dogs is ______________ *(zwischen)* the car and the tree. Bonkers is ______________ *(in)* a bad situation now. Can she get ______________ *(heraus)* it? However, she's not __________ (in) danger, because Mr Miller is coming __________ (heraus) of his house to help her __________ (aus) of this terrible situation.

5 Markiere im Text die Stellen, an denen Präpositionen fehlen. Schreibe die fehlenden Präpositionen in die Spalte neben den Text. Zweimal sind verschiedene Lösungen möglich. ___/25

across (1); *after* (1); *ago* (1); *at* (2); *in* (6); *into* (2), *on* (5); *through* (2); *to* (7); on (1)

It was about 150 years. A big sailing boat sailed the Atlantic Ocean South America. The sun was high the sky and the wind was good. Suddenly the man the mast shouted, "There is another sail there. I can see another ship!" The other sailors (Matrose) went the side of the ship, but the other ship was still too far away.

The afternoon, right lunch, the other ship was so close that they could read the name its side the telescope. It was Tinauticlus. But they couldn't see any people the deck. "They must all be their cabins!" the first mate said the captain.

The evening, before he went his cabin, the captain went the first mate again. He was the steering wheel. "I can't see a person the deck. It's really spooky (gespenstisch)!"

The morning the ship was still their side, so the captain thought, "Let's send some people." He and five sailors took a boat and rowed the ship. They looked every cabin, but the ship was empty! Nobody knows what happened. It is still a mystery.

Some people think the Tinauticlus sailed a storm, others say this ship was a ghost ship its way a dreamworld.

Gesamtpunktzahl _____/113,5

7 Arbeitstechniken und Sprachfertigkeiten

Ein wichtiges Element jeder Sprache sind die in ihr verwendeten Wörter. Deshalb ist die Arbeitstechnik „Wörter lernen" sehr wichtig, auch wenn sie nicht immer auf Begeisterung stößt. Wörter müssen in ihrer Bedeutung, ihrer Schreibweise und ihrer Aussprache gelernt werden.

7.1 Wörter lernen

Regel

Grundsätzliche Hinweise zum Wörterlernen

+ **Lautung:** Sprich jedes neue Wort beim ersten Lernen mehrmals laut aus. Oft sind Begleit-CDs deines Englischbuchs große Hilfen. Bei Ausspracheunsicherheiten kann man neue Wörter am Computer aufnehmen oder ganz einfach jemanden fragen. Die Lautschrift, mit der im Englischbuch die Wörter beschrieben werden, ist ebenfalls hilfreich. Außerdem gibt es im Internet Programme, mit denen man sich die Aussprache „vorlesen" lassen kann.
+ **Schreibung:** Das Vokabelheft, die Vokabelkartei oder der Vokabelordner muss gewissenhaft geführt werden. Jedes neue Wort muss eingetragen werden, am besten gleich, nachdem man es das erste Mal geschrieben oder gelesen hat. Karteikastensysteme gibt es auch von Verlagen. Wichtig ist: Wie du am besten Vokabeln lernst, musst du selbst herausfinden!
+ **Bedeutung:** Lerne Wörter niemals spaltenweise, so wie sie im Buch zu finden sind. Gehe kreuz und quer durch deine Wortliste und von einer Sprache in die andere und umgekehrt. Lerne nicht mechanisch die direkte Übersetzung eines Wortes, sondern versuche, ein neues Wort in einen Sinnzusammenhang zu bringen. Hierzu kann man eine einfache Zeichnung anfertigen oder ein neues Wort im Satzzusammenhang in der Fremdsprache einüben.
  Beispiel: *A lamb is the child of a sheep.* Mit diesem Merksatz hast du gleich zwei neue Wörter *(lamb, sheep)* gelernt.
+ **Wortfelder:** Versuche Wortfelder zu lernen: In Wortfeldern verbindest du sinnverwandte Wörter, Wortfamilien, Wortpaare oder Gegensätze.
  Sinnverwandte Wörter: *to walk (gehen), to run (rennen, laufen) to race (rasen).*
  Wortfamilie: *new (neu), the news (die Nachricht/Nachrichten), to renew (erneuern).*

1 Stelle die folgenden Adjektive mithilfe von Smileys dar.

arrogant	sad	shocked	bored	frightened

Tipp

Jeder Mensch lernt auf eine andere Weise am besten. Daher gibt es verschiedene **Lerntypen**, z. B. den Bildertyp (er zeichnet z. B. Bedeutungen), den Bewegungstyp (er drückt Wörter mit Gesten und anderen Bewegungen aus), den Hörtyp (er spricht Vokabeln laut aus, lernt rhythmisch oder beim Sport), den Schreibtyp (er schreibt, legt Listen oder Mindmaps an) oder den Hingucktyp (er klebt z. B. Zettel mit Wörtern auf den Schreibtisch oder die Pinnwand).
Mit **Mindmaps** („Karten im Kopf") lassen sich Sinnzusammenhänge gut behalten. Dabei werden um einen Begriff Wörter gruppiert, die mit dem Begriff zusammenhängen.

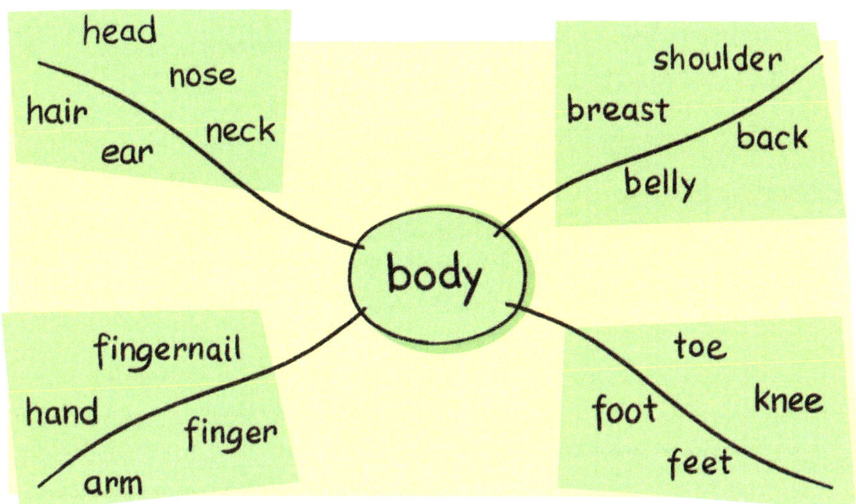

2 Erstelle in deinem Heft eine Mindmap zum Thema *school*. Verwende die aufgelisteten Wörter und ergänze fünf eigene Begriffe.

lesson • subject • timetable • English • Maths • History • class teacher • pupil • test • homework • project • classroom • break • gym • sports ground • headmaster • board • desk • schoolbag.

7.2 Gesprochenes Englisch verstehen

Regel

Richtig zuhören

Es ist ganz normal, dass man in einer Fremdsprache nicht immer jedes gesprochene Wort versteht. Das kann daran liegen, dass dein Gegenüber zu schnell oder einen Dialekt spricht. Dein Hörverstehen muss schließlich erst im Laufe des Sprachenlernens trainiert werden. Hier einige Regeln und Tipps, um die gesprochene Sprache besser zu verstehen.

a) Achte auf die **Gesten** und die **Gesichtsausdrücke** deines Gesprächspartners. Sie können dir Bedeutungen verraten.
b) Werde nicht nervös, wenn du einzelne Teile eines Satzes nicht verstehst. Versuche, die fehlenden Teile aus dem **Zusammenhang** heraus abzuleiten.
c) Teile Deinem Gesprächspartner mit, wenn du etwas nicht verstanden hast. Bitte ihn um langsameres Sprechen. Frage nach und bitte um die **Wiederholung** eines Satzes.
d) Achte auf **Schlüsselwörter** und die Sprechsituation, in der etwas gesagt wird. Sitzt man beispielsweise beim Frühstück und dein Gegenüber fragt *"Do you like porridge?"*, dann verstehst du sicherlich *like* und *Do you*. *Porridge* muss also ziemlich sicher etwas Essbares sein. Lasse dir dann dieses Wort erklären. (Bei *porridge* handelt es sich um eine Art Haferflockenbrei.)

3 Übe mit deinen Familienmitgliedern oder einer Freundin/einem Freund die folgenden Sprechsituationen: Mahlzeiten einnehmen, eine Reise planen, ein Problem in der Familie besprechen, über Schule oder einzelne Fächer diskutieren, über Tagesereignisse sprechen.

4 Heutzutage strahlen viele Radio- und Fernsehsender ihr Programm in ihrer Muttersprache aus. Vielleicht findest du Zeit, dich einmal in einen englischsprachigen Sender einzuklinken. Sei nicht frustriert, wenn du am Anfang wenig verstehst. Mit der Zeit bekommst du immer mehr Bedeutungen mit. Nachrichten in Englisch kannst du z. B. bei CNN oder BBC sehen und hören.

5 Sieh dir deine Lieblingsfilme auf DVD an. Stelle dabei im DVD-Menü als Sprache Englisch und als Untertitel Deutsch ein. Zu einem späteren Zeitpunkt kannst du dir den jeweiligen Film dann auch ohne Untertitel ansehen.

Will man nachfragen, wenn man etwas nicht verstanden hat, bieten sich verschiedene **Standardformulierungen** an:

I'm sorry, I don't/didn't understand. Can you say that again, please?

Can you speak more slowly, please?

Sorry?

Pardon?

Can you please repeat that word/that sentence?

Sorry, can you repeat that?

Would you please explain the meaning of this word to me?

Could you say that again, please?

Sorry, I didn't get that.

Sorry, could you please spell that word?

I beg your pardon, I didn't catch the meaning of this word.

Tipp

Hörverstehenstexte

In Schulaufgaben wird das Hörverstehen meist in Form eines von Muttersprachlern gesprochenen Textes abgeprüft. Um diesen gut verstehen zu können, bieten sich einige Tricks an.

- Hörverstehenstexte handeln fast immer von bekannten Situationen. Daher sollte man beim ersten Hören einfach nur zuhören und versuchen herauszufinden, worum es eigentlich geht. Eine gute Hilfe ist es, dabei die Augen zu schließen und zu versuchen, aus den Worten geistige Bilder zu formen, also sozusagen im Kopf fernzusehen.
- Beim zweiten Hören ist es hilfreich, **Schlüsselbegriffe** zu notieren. Keinesfalls sollte man jedoch versuchen, alles mitzuschreiben, weil man dann beim Zuhören ganz sicher nicht mehr mitkommt und den Faden womöglich komplett verliert.

7.3 Geschriebene Texte verstehen

Regel

Geschriebene Texte verstehen

Wer beim ersten Lesen einen Text nicht vollständig versteht, muss sich keine allzu großen Sorgen machen. Mehrmaliges Lesen führt meist schon zu einem besseren Textverständnis. Für ein genaueres Verständnis gibt es einige hilfreiche Tricks:

Überschriften verdeutlichen das Thema des Textes. **Illustrationen** verraten viel über den Inhalt. **Schlüsselwörter** helfen Teilthemen und Zusammenhänge besser zu verstehen. Nicht jedes unbekannte Wort ist wichtig, Ziel ist es ja, den Text zu verstehen, nicht zu übersetzen. Manche Wörter erschließen sich aus dem **Satz-** oder **Sinnzusammenhang**. Andere Wörter lassen sich **ableiten** (*happy* → *unhappy, happiness*).

Wesentliche Informationen kann man mit den **Wh-Fragen** entnehmen:

Who is the text/the story about?
Where does the story take place?
When does the story happen?
What happens in the story?
Why does it happen?

6 Lese die Geschichte und achte auf die wesentlichen Informationen.

„It is so boring!" Mike is lying on the beach. He is on holiday in Greece with his parents. They are sitting behind him in the restaurant at the hotel pool and are laughing and having fun. They met some people at the disco the night before and had dinner with them, and now everybody is telling jokes, boring jokes.

Mike feels so alone. The hotel is five kilometers from the next town and there are no other young people - except two girls! They giggle all the time, especially when they look at him and they can't even speak English! One of them must be 13, like Mike, and the other one, the dark-haired one, that looks a little like Shakira, must be a little younger. She's got brown eyes and she smiles all the time. They must be from Germany, because on their bag there is a German flag, black, red and gold stripes. Mike has got the Union Jack on his rucksack. "Mike, why are you looking so miffed? Do something! No wonder you feel bored!"

Mothers can be terrible! Why does she always have to shout things all over the beach?

He is sure that the girls are looking at him, but he doesn't look in their direction. Mike is trying not to blush. He's hoping the girls are in the water. Mike peeks in their direction and is very happy not to be able to see them. After some time he stands up, takes his diving mask and snorkel and goes to the sea. Slowly, very slowly. Cool in the sun!

Just when he steps into the water, he sees the girls. They are swimming right in front of him when one of them, the younger one, suddenly screams, *"Autsch! Mich hat 'was gebissen!"* The girls swim to the beach and sit down right next to him. He can see that there is blood on the girl's foot. *"Hast du ein Taschentuch?"* the older girl asks him. - "Sorry, I don't understand!" - "A tissue! A hankie?" - "I'll get one from my rucksack," says Mike and rushes back to his chair. They can speak English. They must have understood everything his mother had said. What a shame! "Here you are - some tissues! I brought some band-aid, too!" - "Thank you!", says Shakira (?), "I'm Nicole (!), but call me Niki (!!). Can you have a look? By the way, what's your name?" - "My name ...", Mike is stammering a bit, "... is Mike. How do you do?" Carefully he looks at Shakira's, no, Niki's foot. "It's a small cut, not very deep. It doesn't look like a bite or so. Maybe you've stepped onto a piece of broken glass. But it looks clean. We'll stick some band-aid on it and it'll be all right in a few days. But if you want, my dad can look at it. He's a doctor and he's sitting in the restaurant over there." - "I know, our parents are with him." - "They seem to be having a lot of fun," Mike says when he suddenly hears some loud laughter from the restaurant.

"I hope I can ride my bike this afternoon," Niki says, "we want to go into town this afternoon. There's the new James Bond at the cinema, not in Greek but in English. What are you going to do this afternoon, Mike?" - "Nothing, really!" - "Why don't you come with us? We can rent another bike at the hotel!" - "Okay!" - "Hey, if you come with us, we won't have to be back at the hotel so early! Let's tell our parents." Life can be so wonderful!

7 Kreuze an, ob die Antwort korrekt oder falsch ist.

	true	false
a) Mike is on holiday with his aunt and uncle.		
b) They are in Germany.		
c) There are a lot of young people at the hotel.		
d) Shakira is also at their hotel.		
e) Shakira has got the Union Jack on her bag.		
f) Mike's mother is from Germany.		
g) She is very loud, so Mike is sometimes embarrassed.		

	true	false
h) When you are embarrassed, you blush. This means you become red in your face.		
i) Niki stepped onto a broken bottle.		
j) Mike has got some tissues in his rucksack.		
k) 'Self-conscious' has got the same meaning as 'embarrassed'.		
l) Mike is going to go to the cinema alone.		
m) He is happy in the end.		
n) There was laughter from the restaurant.		
o) The new James Bond film is in Greek.		
p) One of the parents is a doctor.		

Info plus

Die britische Flagge heißt ***Union Jack***, weil sie symbolisch die Union zwischen England, Schottland und Nordirland darstellt. Die *Union Flag*, so der offizielle Name, ist seit 1809 Nationalflagge. Auf der Flagge werden auf weißem Grund das rote Kreuz des englischen Nationalheiligen St. George, auf blauem Grund das weiße Kreuz des schottischen Nationalheiligen St. Andrew und auf weißem Grund das rote Kreuz des irischen Nationalheiligen St. Patrick miteinander kombiniert.

Zahlreiche ehemalige Kolonien bilden in ihren Nationalflaggen ebenfalls die britische Flagge ab, zum Beispiel Australien und Neuseeland.

Tipp

Fragen

- Fragen werden am besten immer in der **Zeitform** beantwortet, in der sie gestellt werden. Wenn also die Frage lautet *"Why did Niki scream?"*, muss die Antwort lauten *"She screamed because she felt some pain on her foot."*
- Ganz wichtig ist, dass man bei Fragen mit Fragewörtern nicht vergisst, **ganze Sätze** zu bilden. Lautet die Antwort auf obige Frage nur *"Because she stepped onto a broken bottle."*, fehlt der Haupsatz. Dies ist im gesprochenen Englisch kein Problem, im geschriebenen Englisch aber kann es ein Fehler sein. Besonders oft passiert dies bei Fragen mit dem Fragewort *Why*.
- **Beginne** deshalb im geschriebenen Englisch einen Satz **nie mit *Because*** …, sondern wiederhole die Frage als Aussage und füge anschließend die Begründung hinzu.

8 Beantworte die folgenden Fragen zum Text in ganzen Sätzen.

a) Who are the people in the story? ______

b) Where does the story take place? ______

c) Where do the girls come from? ______

d) Where are Mike's parents while he is on the beach? ______

e) Why is Mike so bored? ______

f) Why is Mike embarrassed? ______

g) What happens when Mike is walking to the sea? ______

h) Why did Niki scream? ______

i) Why can't Mike understand Niki? ______

j) Where do they plan to go to in the afternoon? ______

k) How can we see that Mike likes Niki? ______

l) Does the story have a happy ending? ______

7.4 Einfache Sprechsituationen

Regel

Sich und andere vorstellen

- Wenn man sich oder andere Personen vorstellen will, kann man die folgenden **Phrasen** verwenden:
  May I introduce myself. My name is Albert Einstein. - Darf ich mich vorstellen. Ich heiße Albert Einstein.
  oder: *May I introduce Mary to you? Mr. X, this is Mary Longman, Mary this is Mr. X. - Darf ich Ihnen Mary vorstellen? Herr X, das ist Mary, Mary, das ist Mr. X.*
- Wer seinem Gegenüber **weitere Informationen** über sich geben möchte, kann die folgenden Phrasen verwenden:
  Alter: *I'm 12 years old./I'm 12.*
  Herkunft: *I'm from Augsburg, a town in the south of Germany.*
  Hobbys: *I like/love tennis, hockey and playing chess.*

9 Gib deinem Gesprächspartner alle Informationen in ganzen Sätzen.

a) Doris
age: 14; from Hamburg (in the north of Germany); hobbies: swimming, reading books, chess and dancing

Hi, I'm …

b) Mr Wagner
age: very old; from Augsburg (60 km northwest of Munich); hobbies: playing the guitar, working with drama groups; writing English books

May I introduce myself …

Wünsche und Abneigungen äußern

Wenn man etwas gerne tut oder mag, kann man die folgenden Verben verwenden:
like - wollen, mögen, gerne haben
oder *love* - sehr gerne haben, lieben.

I like chess.
- Ich mag Schach.

He likes/loves swimming.
- Er schwimmt (sehr) gerne.

Wenn man etwas nicht gerne tut oder gar hasst, kann man die Verneinungen von *like/love* verwenden oder die Verben *dislike/hate*.

He doesn't like/love writing tests.

We dislike her brother.

They hate mowing the lawn.

Wenn man eine Sache oder eine Tätigkeit einer anderen Sache bzw. Tätigkeit vorzieht, kann man das Verb *prefer to* (vorziehen) verwenden.

She prefers tea to coffee.

I prefer listening to pop music to watching boring films.

Favourite ist ein passendes Wort, um seine Vorlieben auszudrücken.

My favourite hobby is playing the violine.

Our favourite movie is 'Harry Potter and the Order of the Phoenix'.

10 Schreibe auf, was die Personen gerne mögen/tun, vorziehen, am liebsten mögen oder nicht mögen.

a)

I don't like ______, but I ______________________

b)

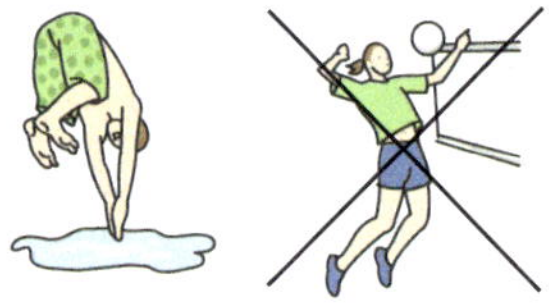

He prefers ______________________

c)

I hate ______________________

____

d)

He dislikes ______________________

____

e) favourite animal:

My ______________________

f) Sarah's favourite song: "Bleeding love"

Her ______________________

____

g)

Peter doesn't ______________________

____

h)

Susan ______________________

____

i)

My parents don't ______________________

11 Schreibe auf, was du gerne magst oder tust, was du vorziehst, am liebsten magst oder gar nicht gerne tust.
Verwende die Verben *like, dislike, love, hate* und *prefer*.

70 Welche Alternativen zum Erlernen von Wörtern gibt es neben der Arbeit mit Wortlisten? ______________________________

____

71 Welche drei „Eigenschaften" musst du bei einem neuen Wort lernen?

____

72 Welche Begriffsuntergruppen zum Thema *Christmas* lassen sich in einer Mindmap bilden? ______________________________

____

73 Was sagst du deinem Gegenüber, wenn du ewas nicht verstanden hast?

____

74 – **78** Liste die wh-Wörter auf, mit denen du nach den Inhalten eines Textes fragst.

74 ____________ **75** ____________ **76** ____________

77 ____________ **78** ____________

79 Mit welchen Sätzen kannst du dich vorstellen?

____

80 Wie fragst du nach dem Alter deines Gesprächspartners?

____

81 – **83** Welche Verben drücken das Nicht-Mögen bzw. eine Ablehnung aus?

81 ______________________________

82 ______________________________

83 ______________________________

84 Welcher Wortzusatz sagt aus, dass jemand etwas besonders gerne mag?

____

1 Arbeite mit einem Wörterbuch und finde die fehlenden Ableitungen. Schreibe auch die deutschen Bedeutungen dazu. ___/13

Verb	Adjektiv	Nomen
renew		
	shocking	
		slowness
	introductory	
favour		
	understandable	
		happiness

2 Vervollständige die Mindmap. ___/7

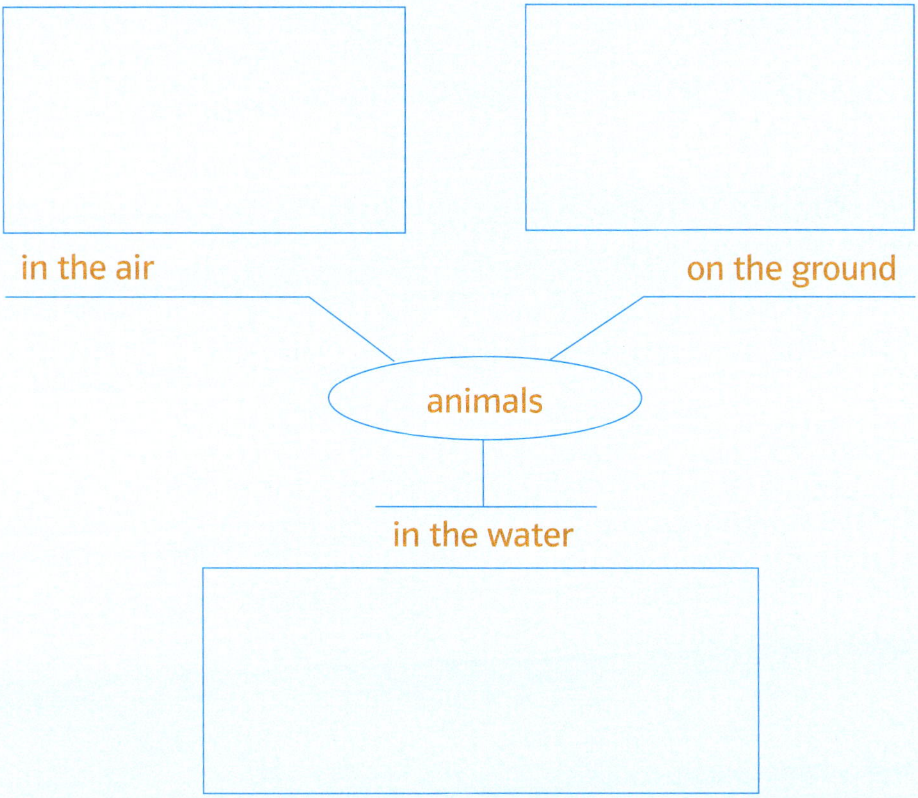

___/16 **3** Beantworte jede Frage zum Text in einem vollständigen Satz. Verwende zur Klärung ein Wörterbuch oder ein Online-Lexikon.

Bavaria Wildlife Park

Our zoo is one of the most popular leisure facilities in Germany. It has seventy species of mammals and more than two hundred species of birds and interesting reptiles, amphibians and insects. The animals live in spacious outdoor enclosures on an area of about 70000 acres. Along our walkways you find a Jungle Restaurant, a big adventure playground, shady trees, our information centre, open meadows and many ponds. We can offer you guided tours through various areas, and in our information centre you can get information about wildlife and the threat to endangered animals. Our zoo supports many projects which protect endangered species in their natural habitats. Come and visit us, and show your interest for nature.

Opening hours:
9.00 am to 6.00 pm: April to September
9.00 am to 5.00 pm: October and March
9.00 am to 4.30 pm: November to February

Admission fees:
adults: 8 €
child (3 to 14): 4 €, free under 3
family ticket: 18 €

a) What kind of animals does Bavaria Wildlife Park present?

____

____

b) How big is the wildlife area?

____

c) Where can you have a meal?

____

d) What type of information can you get in the information centre?

____

e) How does the zoo support endangered species?

____

f) Why can't you stay until 6.00 pm in February?

____

g) What is the admission fee for three adults?

____

h) How much must two families pay?

____

4 Übersetze. ___/16

a) Darf ich Ihnen meine Schwester vorstellen?

____

b) Ich komme aus München, einer Stadt im Süden Bayerns.

____

c) Mein Hobby sind Bücher und ich mag auch Basketball sehr gerne.

____

d) Unser Lieblingslehrer heißt Thomas Cook.

____

e) Könnten Sie diesen Satz bitte noch einmal wiederholen?

____

f) Könnten Sie bitte etwas langsamer sprechen?

____

g) Entschuldigung, könnten Sie dieses Wort bitte buchstabieren?

____

h) Ich mag Englisch, aber Mathematik mag ich nicht.

____

Gesamtpunktzahl ______/52

Kannst du diese Fragen am Ende der Klasse 5 problemlos beantworten? In Klasse 6 wird vorausgesetzt, dass du diese Regeln sicher beherrschst.

85 Warum ist das Grundmuster P-O-S für den englischen Aussagesatz falsch?

____

86 Wann wird die Verlaufsform des Präsens *(present progressive)* verwendet?

____

87 Wann wird die einfache Form des Präsens *(simple present)* verwendet?

____

88 Welche Hilfskonstruktionen braucht man bei der Verneinung des *simple present*?

____

89 Wie heißen die *simple past*-Formen der Verben *do*, *buy* und *sleep*?

____

90 Welche beiden Formen, die Zukunft auszudrücken, kennst du bereits? Wie unterscheidet sich ihr Gebrauch?

____

____

91 Worin liegt der Unterschied zwischen *much* und *many*?

____

____

92 Was ist bei der Schreibweise von Nomen und Adjektiven, die Länder bezeichnen, im Englischen immer zu beachten?

____

____

93 Wie unterscheiden sich Adjektive und Adverbien im Hinblick auf ihr Bezugswort?

94 Wie nennt man die Adverbien des Ortes, der Zeit und der Richtung im Englischen?

95 Wie werden die Präpositionen *auf*, *unter*, *neben*, *vor* und *hinter* ins Englische übersetzt?

96 Welche Zeitpräposition zeigt einen Zeitraum vor dem Moment des Sprechens an?

97 Welchen Genitiv benutzt man, wenn das Bezugswort keine Person ist?

98 Warum ist es wenig sinnvoll, Wörter spaltenweise zu lernen?

99 Du hast einen englischen Satz nicht verstanden. Würdest du *"Say it again!"* sagen? Begründe.

Kapitel 1: Grundlegende Satzbausteine

Aufgaben

Seite 7

1 a) Meine Eltern lesen Zeitungen./My parents read newspapers.
b) Können wir diese Geschichte erzählen?/Can we tell this story?
c) Du liebst italienisches Essen./You love Italian food.
d) Die Katze meines Freundes frisst Mäuse./My friend's cat eats mice.

2 a) Dr. Sixt meets Dr. First. b) She watches TV. c) Beyoncé sings good songs.
d) My dog hates cats. e) Mike reads comics. f) Sarah likes Latin.
g) Peter writes letters.

Seite 8

3 a) I am (I'm) nervous. b) You are (You're) old. c) He is (He's) fast.
d) She is (She's) excited. e) It is (It's) rainy. f) We are (We're) happy.
g) You are (You're) sad. h) They are (They're) tired.

Seite 9

4 b) We aren't strong. We're not strong.
c) You aren't a boy. You're not a boy.
d) I'm not a girl.
e) Susan isn't late. Susan's not late.
f) Tom and Paul aren't here. They're not here.
g) It isn't cold. It's not cold.
h) You aren't tired. You're not tired.
i) She isn't Irish. She's not Irish.
j) It isn't too late. It's not too late.
k) They aren't angry. They're not angry.
l) I'm not hungry.

Seite 10

5 b) The house isn't big, it's small.
c) Mr and Mrs Miller aren't here, they're over there.
d) Peter isn't tall, he's short.
e) You aren't nine, you're ten.
f) The girl isn't good at Maths or History, she's very good at English.

Seite 11

6

dt. (Aussagesatz)	engl. (Frage, bejaht)	engl. (Frage, verneint)	engl. (Frage, verneint, Kurzform)
Du bist klug.	Are you clever?	Are you not clever?	Aren't you clever?
Mary ist komisch.	Is Mary funny?	**Is Mary not funny?**	**Isn't Mary funny?**
Mein Vater ist Lehrer.	**Is my father a teacher?**	Is my father not a teacher?	Isn't my father a teacher?
Die Jungen sind spät dran.	**Are the boys late?**	Are the boys not late?	**Aren't the boys late?**
Er ist aufgeregt.	**Is he excited?**	**Is he not excited?**	**Isn't he excited?**

Seite 12

7 a) No, Mum, **I'm not**. b) No, **they aren't**. c) Yes, **he is**.
d) Oh yes, **we are**. e) No, **I'm not**. f) No, **she isn't**.

8 Unterschiedliche Antworten sind möglich. Beispiele:
a) Is Susan ten?
b) Are Peter and Paul from London?
c) Are you Irish?
d) Are you an English teacher?
e) Is it Monday today?
f) Is Max from Birmingham?

9 dein Lineal – **your ruler**; seine Eltern – **his parents**; euer Haus – **your house**; mein Leben – **my life**; ihre Kinder – **their children**; ihre Schwester – **her sister/their sister**; unsere Schule – **our school**; ihr Bruder – **her brother/their brother**; eure Frage – **your question**; meine Antwort – **my answer** **Seite 13**

10 a) Lea's cat. **Seite 14/15**
b) Mr and Mrs Hall's car.
c) His uncle's books.
d) The Millers' house.
e) Frank's dog.
f) Her child's bike.
g) Her brother's computer.
h) Their children's skateboards.
i) Our teacher's football.

11 This is my aunt's, Mrs. Dexter's, house. Her son's bike is in front of the garage with her husband's car. Her daughter's dog always sleeps in the garden. The family's home is in Oak Road. My aunt works outside the town. She works at the hospital. My aunt's children know this hospital well. **Seite 15**

12 a) The mayor of the town **Seite 15/16**
b) The market of Camden Town
c) The colour of the bus
d) The windows of Westminster Abbey
e) The age of the Crown Jewels
f) The length of Tower Bridge
g) The depth of the river Thames
h) The size of Hyde Park
i) The sound of Big Ben
j) The lines of the Tube
k) The towers of the Tower

13 a) The bells of the church **Seite 16/17**
b) The owner of the house
c) The price of the car
d) The saddle of the bike
e) The age of the TV set
f) The height of the tree
g) The roofs of the huts
h) The top of the mountain

14 a) **These are** terrible pictures, but **those are** wonderful posters. **Seite 17**
b) **This is** a nice car, but **that is** an ugly old camper.
c) **Is this** here a new bike? – No, but **that is** a new one over there.
d) **Are these** cheap pencils? – Yes, and **those are** cheap pencils over there, too.

15 Julia: **Seite 18**
"**These** people here are my parents, and **those** boys over there are my brothers."
"**This** building here is my parents' house, and **that** house over there is our neighbour's house."
"**This** person on the right is my grandma. This person here next to her is my grandpa"
"**That** cat over there is Sally. And **this** dog here is our dog Barkey."
"**That** horse over there is our neighbours' horse. His name is Fury."
"And **that** tree over there is his favourite apple tree. Fury likes to eat **those** apples over there."

Seite 19

16 a) Please give me the book.
b) Don't tell him the story.
c) Write her a letter.
d) Put it (the exercise book) on the table.

Seite 20

17 a) Look, Dorothee is in **her** room. **She**'s happy. **Her** neighbours are in **their** garden. **They**'re very happy, too.
b) Steve is thirteen. **He**'s not twelve. **He**'s looking at me. **I**'m his friend. **My** (oder: **His**) bike is new, **I** like **it** very much.
c) Jane: "Fred and his sister are at home this afternoon. Can **you** please call **them** at five o'clock?" - Dan: "Yes, **I** can. But **I** must first do **my** homework."
d) "Don't touch **me**, Pete. **I**'m in a bad mood."
e) **My** parents are in **their** garage. **They**'re washing **their** car.

18 a) Is there cheese in the fridge?
b) There is a famous TV tower in Berlin.
c) There are six pencils on the table.
d) There are many problems.

Seite 21

19 a) It's; his; he's
b) there's; your
c) you're
d) It's; its
e) They're
f) Their
g) it's
h) he's
i) It's

Seite 22

20 a) My brother has got two birds.
b) Has he got his exercise books at home?
c) Have you got my pencil?
d) Have your parents got two cars?

Seite 23

21 a) He hasn't got much time.
b) Haven't you got a sister?
c) They haven't got a tree in their garden.
d) My aunt hasn't got a big family.

22 a) No, they haven't. b) Yes, she has. c) No, I haven't. d) Yes, they have.

23 Mehrere Sätze sind möglich, z. B.: Tim writes letters. My father tells stories. Our teacher looks at me. We know much. Her sisters read comics. Her sisters know much. etc.

Seite 24

Training plus

1 Nach dem Objekt eines Satzes fragt man mit „wem", „wen" oder „was".

2 Subjektfall: *I, you, he, she, it, we, you, they.*
Objektfall: *me, you, him, her, it, us, you, them.*

3 Verneinte Kurzformen von be: *isn't, aren't*.

4 *They're* ist die Kurzform von *they are* (sie sind), *their* ist das Possessivpronomen (3. Person Plural). *He's* ist die Kurzform von *He is* (Er ist), *his* ist das Possessivpronomen (3. Person Singular, männlich).

5 s-Genitiv

6 *these* bezieht sich auf Dinge in der Nähe, *those* auf solche weiter weg oder Dinge von geringerer Bedeutung.

7 Übersetzung von *there is/there are*: Es gibt ...

8 Immer dann, wenn jemandem etwas gehört oder wenn etwas auf ihn bezogen wird.

9 *hasn't got* und *haven't got*

10 S - P - O *(subject - predicate - object)*

Abschlusstest

Allgemeine Hinweise zum Abschlusstest
Damit du deine Gesamtpunktzahl einfach errechnen kannst, gibt es für jede Teilaufgabe bei Lückenaufgaben in der Regel einen Punkt, bei Übersetzungsaufgaben oder schwierigeren Aufgaben zwei Punkte.
Leider ist es nicht möglich, einen allgemeingültigen Notenschlüssel vorzugeben. Er wechselt von Schule zu Schule, von Bundesland zu Bundesland. Damit du deine Leistung einschätzen kannst, gibt es folgende Orientierungspunkte:
- Wenn du mehr als 80 Prozent der Gesamtpunktzahl erreicht hast, ist dein Ergebnis gut oder besser.
- Wenn du mehr als 50 Prozent der Gesamtpunktzahl erreicht hast, ist dein Ergebnis ausreichend oder befriedigend.
- Wenn du weniger als 50 Prozent der Gesamtpunktzahl erreicht hast, ist dein Ergebnis nicht mehr ausreichend. Du solltest dann die Regeln und Aufgaben, bei denen du viele Fehler gemacht hast, noch einmal genau nachlesen und üben.

Seite 25

100 bis 80 Prozent	79 bis 50 Prozent	unter 50 Prozent
sehr gut bis gut	befriedigend bis ausreichend	nicht mehr ausreichend

1 Mike is my sister's hamster. He's two years old. His ears are white and his eyes are brown. Is he a "he" or a "she"? He's a male hamster. My sister's very happy with Mike. She's a pet lover. She's also very interested in cats. __/16

2 **My** uncle is an English teacher. The name of **his** school is Barton Comprehensive. **He** likes English ghost stories very much. **I** like adventure stories. **My** favourite subjects at school are Maths and Arts. Our Arts teacher is a wonderful man. **He**'s young and **his** lessons are so interesting. I like **him** and he likes **me**. __/10

3 a) I'm not lazy. b) She's not ten/She isn't ten.
c) Isn't he tall? d) Aren't we poor?
e) They aren't at school. They're not at school. __/5

Seite 26

4 a) Yes, **she has**. b) No, **he isn't**. c) No, **they haven't**.
d) Yes, **they are**. e) No, **I'm not**. __/5

5 a) Our **children's** hobby is very expensive. b) The **lamp of my bike** is brand new.
c) Peter**'s** goldfish is over eight years old. d) **My parents'** car is a 1999 Chevrolet.
e) He likes **the colour of our house**. __/5

6 a) Open your books.
b) Don't speak in/during the lesson.
c) Sarah, help him.
d) Say it/that again.
e) Don't do your homework now.
f) Give me the heavy bag.
g) Sit down.
h) Don't look at your neighbour.
i) Put the pencil case on the table.
j) Don't sleep.

___/20

Seite 27

7 a) ~~There's~~ → **There are** so many nice pupils in our new class.
b) ~~Have~~ → **Has** your mum got much time for her hobbies?
c) ~~he's fathers~~ → The young girl likes **her father's** new DVDs.
d) ~~is'nt;~~ → He **isn't** interested in football. ~~he's~~ → He likes **his** basketball team.
e) ~~Its~~ → **It's** Saturday afternoon … ~~their's~~ → and **there's** the news on TV.
f) ~~this~~ → Look at **these** people. ~~Their~~ → **They're** really nasty.

___/6

8 a) Have you got money for a new CD, Sue?
b) Close the windows and the doors, Pete.
c) I'm not a pupil at my father's school, Mr Lewis.
d) Don't call me 'donkey', Jack.
e) Has your sister got the measles, Jim?

___/10

77 – 62 Punkte	61 – 39 Punkte	unter 39 Punkte
sehr gut bis gut	befriedigend bis ausreichend	nicht mehr ausreichend

___/77

Kapitel 2: Verben: Zeitformen der Gegenwart

Aufgaben

Seite 28

1

I play	I write	I put	I buy	I watch	I hurry
you play	you write	you put	you buy	you watch	you hurry
he plays	he writes	he puts	he buys	he watches	he hurries
we play	we write	we put	we buy	we watch	we hurry
you play	you write	you put	you buy	you watch	you hurry
they play	they write	they put	they buy	they watch	they hurry

Seite 29

2 On schooldays, I **get up** at seven o'clock. Then I **go** to the bathroom and **wash** myself. My brother **gets up** later. His school **starts** at nine. My sister is also still in bed. She **goes** to university in Liverpool and often **works** very late. After breakfast, I **brush** my teeth and then I **take** the number 8 bus to school. My friends Tom and Trish usually **wait** for me in front of the school. They **are** brother and sister.

Seite 30

3 Every Sunday Bianca gets up late. After breakfast, she **takes** a shower and then she **sits** down in the living room and **watches** a show on TV. Then she **helps** her mom in the kitchen. She **puts** forks, knives and plates on the table and **fetches** some wine for her father from the cellar. In the afternoon, Bianca and her parents **go** for a walk to the park or, if the weather is bad, they **play** 'Settlers of Catan'. Sometimes they also **have** visitors. Bianca's grandpa sometimes **comes** for tea. He usually **brings** a cake. Bianca **calls** it "The best cake in the world!". In the evening, Bianca **does** her homework and later she **watches** TV or reads a book. She usually **goes** to bed at nine o'clock because she **gets up** very early on schooldays. She **lives** in a small village and **takes** the bus to school. The bus **leaves** every morning at seven o'clock.

4 In Germany, school doesn't start at 8.45. Pupils don't have assembly. Lessons don't last for 50 minutes. After four lessons, pupils don't go for lunch. German pupils don't have lessons every afternoon. School in Germany usually doesn't end at 3.15. German pupils don't do their homework then. **Seite 31**

5 a) He doesn't lie to her. b) She doesn't believe him. c) "Don't you miss me?"
d) "I don't always love you." e) "He doesn't have another girlfriend."
f) "I don't like him." g) He doesn't leave her. h) She doesn't forget him.

6 a) Does my father work in the garden every weekend? – Yes, he does. **Seite 32**
b) Does my father help in the kitchen whenever he can? – No, he doesn't.
c) Do Tom and Linda play tennis every afternoon? – Yes, they do.
d) Don't they do their homework? – No, they don't.
e) Do we read comics in the morning? – No, we don't.

7 a) When **does Bianca get up** every Sunday? **Seite 33/34**
b) When **does she take** a shower?
c) What **does she do** after her shower?
d) What **does she put** on the table?
e) Where **does she go** for a walk?
f) When **do they play** 'Settlers of Catan'?
g) Who **comes for tea** sometimes?
h) What **does Bianca** call it?
i) When **does she do** her homework on Sundays?
j) When **does she go** to bed?
k) Why **does she go** to bed at nine o'clock?
l) Where **does she** live?
m) How **does she get** to school?
n) When **does the bus** leave every morning?
o) What **do** you think about this exercise?
p) What do you **do** to improve your English?
q) What **do** we say?

8 a) Where are Tom and Mike? **Seite 34**
b) Who is Jenny's German friend?
c) Have your parents got a TV in their bedroom?
d) Is there a toilet downstairs?
e) How old are you?

9 a) He **is** (He's) **coming** home. **Seite 35/36**
b) They **are** (They're) **cleaning** their rooms.
c) She **is** (She's) **shutting** the window.
d) We **are** (We're) **talking** much at the moment.
e) He **is** (He's) **putting** the pen on the desk.
f) You **are** (You're) **reading** the newspaper.
g) She **is** (She's) **writing** a letter to her friend.
h) It **is** (It's) **getting** hot.
i) I **am** (I'm) **buying** a new bike.

10 A man **is sitting** on a bench. He **is reading** a newspaper. A dog **is sniffing** at the man's leg. Two girls **are riding** their bikes. They **are laughing** about the man. A bird **is flying** in the air. Another bird **is singing** in a tree. A little girl **is having** an ice cream. A boy **is standing** next **Seite 36/37**

to her. He wants an ice cream, too, so he **is pulling** at his mother's arm. The boy's mother **is talking** to another woman. The two women **are smiling**.

Seite 37/38

11 Yes, Mike **is sitting** alone over there. He **never plays** with the boys. And Julia and Hanna **are talking**. They **usually talk** a lot. And Elly **is coming** back from the toilet. She **goes** to the toilet every lesson. But Sandy **never sits** alone, only sometimes. But then, she **has always got** trouble with her boyfriend.

Seite 38

12 a) Mike goes to a snackbar every friday after work./Every Friday after work Mike goes to a snackbar.
b) He has a sandwich then.
c) Sandra is coming. She's smiling.
d) She's happy because today is a special day.
e) Mike usually takes Sandra home in his car.
f) They are staying in town until nine o'clock because it's Sandra's birthday.
g) They go to the cinema and watch a movie with Leonardo di Caprio.
h) They don't go to the disco.

Seite 39

Training plus

11 … wenn etwas immer wieder so geschieht und wenn Handlungen neu einsetzen.

12 *present progressive*

13 *simple present*

14 *present progressive*

15 *He, she, it,* das **s** muss mit.

16 z.B. *always, often, sometimes*

17 auf *-ied*

18 *he goes, she does, he buys*

19 *has not got (hasn't got)*

20 gerade

21 S - P - O, kein Unterschied zum deutschen Aussagesatz.

Seite 40/41

Abschlusstest

1 Hello, my name **is** Dopey, one of the 7 dwarfs. I **usually live** 'Beyond the Seven Hills', but I **am living** in the Alps at the moment. I **go** to work in the goldmine every day, but I **am not working** at the moment, because I **am** on holiday. My friend Grumpy **is sitting** over there. He **does not feel** happy, so he **is shouting** at Doc. Grumpy **always shouts** at us. I **never shout** at my friends. They all **like** me but they **do not like** Grumpy.

___/15

2 a) Where are you from?
b) How old are you?
c) Have you got a pet?
d) Do you like singing and laughing?
e) Does Grumpy love songs?
f) How many girlfriends and how many boyfriends have you got?
g) Is Snow White a dwarf?
h) Why does she live with you? ___/9

3 a) I like fairy tales and I'm reading a book about the Brothers Grimm. Seite 41
b) These storytellers are very popular in Germany.
c) Everybody knows them. Their stories are exciting and interesting.
d) At school we're talking about Wilhelm Busch.
e) This author is famous for his poems and funny rhymes.
f) Many people know his stories about/of Max and Moritz. ___/12

36 – 29 Punkte	28 – 18 Punkte	unter 18 Punkte
sehr gut bis gut	befriedigend bis ausreichend	nicht mehr ausreichend

___/36

Kapitel 3: Verben: Zeitformen der Vergangenheit und Zukunft

Aufgaben

1 Tina worked. They played. We asked. She answered. I watched. Tom visited. They talked. You wanted. She liked. He cleaned. It rained. I jumped. I looked. They hurried. Seite 43

2 a) I was ill.
b) You were on holiday.
c) We were in school.
d) He was hungry.

4 Last Saturday my grandfather did not (didn't) go for a walk late in the afternoon. After teatime he did not (didn't) play chess with his neighbour and then he did not (didn't) listen to the evening news on the radio. After that he did not (didn't) help his wife in the kitchen. He did not (didn't) clean the table and he did not (didn't) go to bed and read a book. And on Sunday he never got up (did not get/didn't get) early and he never went (did not go/didn't go) to church. At lunchtime he never went (did not go; didn't go) to an Italian restaurant. Seite 45

5 Yesterday Patrick **had** an exciting adventure. In the afternoon he **rode** his bike along Baker Street and **saw** two men in black masks next to the bank. At once Patrick **jumped** off his bike and **hid** behind a phone box. Slowly he **opened** the heavy door of the phone box. "I just hope they won't notice me", he **thought**. "I must call the police." But suddenly the bank robbers **came** out of the bank. They **raced** away in their car with screeching tyres. Patrick **tried** to see their number plate OXJ 63..? Then he **heard** the sirens of the police cars. When the four police officers **got** out of their cars, Patrick **said**: "I **saw** part of their number plate." He **felt** very proud. Seite 46

6 going to-future: I **am (I'm) going to** play football. She **is (She's) going to** go home soon. We **are (We're) going to** win this match. It **is (It's) going to** snow. Seite 47
Will-future: He **will (He'll)** visit his aunt in London. You **will (You'll)** know the story. They **will (They'll)** tell you everything. She **will (She'll)** phone you.

Seite 48 7 Bianca **will be** thirteen next Friday. She **is going to** invite all her friends to her house, and hopefully everybody **will have** a lot of fun. They **are going to** dance to their favourite music, and Bianca's mother **is going to** prepare some delicious snacks. Bianca's grandparents **will not** come. The music **will be** much too loud for them. Nobody knows whether the sun **will** shine, that's why Bianca **is going to** have a party in the garage. There they can be as loud as they like and they **will not (won't)** bother any neighbours. Annika and Verena, Bianca's best friends, **are going to** give her a great birthday present: a concert ticket for her favourite band. The concert **will be** in August. They **are not going to** go to this concert, as they aren't too fond of 'Green Day' themselves.

Seite 50 8 "Mum, **can I go** to Verena's home?" - "Sorry, Bianca, I'm on the telephone. **Can you** ask me later?" - "But, Mum, I **must ask** her about my homework! If I don't go now, she …" - "I told you I'm on the phone. I will have time for you in a minute. You **must not (mustn't)** shout at me!" - "Oh, Mum, **can't you talk** to your friend later?" - "That's it, Bianca. I told you you **must not (mustn't)** disturb me on the phone. So you **cannot/can't** go to Verena's home today. You **can call** her about your homework." - "But I **can't call**! You started your call two hours ago!"

9 Bianca was grounded. Now she has to do her homework alone. She mustn't call her friends. She mustn't leave the house. She must go to bed early. She mustn't watch TV. She must read all the time. She mustn't beat her little brother. She must clean the table. She must wash the dishes. She must learn the vocabulary.

Seite 51 **Training plus**

22 *auxiliaries*

23 z. B. *can, must, need to*

24 Hilfsverben können nicht alleine auftreten, sie benötigen ein Vollverb.

25 *-ed*

26 Es gibt keinen, die Formen des Verbs sind identisch.

27 Bei Handlungen und Zuständen, die abgeschlossen in der Vergangenheit liegen.

28 Das *-y* der Grundform wird zu *-ied* im simple past.

29 *took, went, drove*

30 Das geschriebene *-ed* wird [id] ausgesprochen.

31 *was, were*

32 *need not (needn't), don't/doesn't have to*

Seite 52 **Abschlusstest**

1 a) Tim: "**May** I feed the cat, please?" b) Mother: "No, but you **can** wash the dishes."
___/3 c) Tim: "Why **must** I always do the dirty work?"

2 Bianca's grandpa **will be** 86 soon. He **is going to** have a super party on his birthday. He **is going to invite** Bianca, her parents and all his other friends. He hopes they **will come** to his party. He **is going to bake** a big cake for his guests. But he **will not invite** his neighbour. ___/6

3 One day, when Grumpy and his friends **came** home from the mines they **found** their house in a terrible mess. They **went** upstairs and then they **saw** it. Dopey **asked**, "Who **slept** in my bed?" "I'm **going to hit** the person very hard!", **said** Grumpy. He and Doc **were** angry because their food **was** gone. But then Snow White **lived** with the dwarfs, and they all **fell** in love with her. But they **warned** her, "Your evil stepmother **doesn't like** you. She **will put** on a disguise and **will try** to kill you, Snow White. You **must be** very careful!", they **said**. And so it **happened**. Twice the dwarfs **found** her on time, but the third time they **were** late. When they **came** home, Doc **asked**, "Snow White, where **are** you?" "She **is lying** on the ground!", Dopey **said** and **started** to cry. ___/27

4 **Seite 53**
a) Last year Mr Johnson ~~doesn't~~ move to Brighton. → didn't
b) ~~Doesn't~~ he have a car accident last week? → Didn't
c) After school George ~~goed~~ to his aunt's house. → went
d) Peter and Susan ~~was~~ reading the Sunday newspaper. → were
e) Tom: "The past tense form of 'buy' is '~~buyed~~'". → bought
f) Sue: " Must I read this book?" - Dad: "No, you ~~mustn't~~." → needn't/don't have to
g) Max ~~are~~ going to go on holiday to France next month. → is
h) ~~Haven't~~ she got a new bike? → Hasn't
i) This movie is very old. They ~~make~~ it in 1960. → made
j) Must I post this letter? - No, you ~~must~~. → needn't/don't have to ___/10

46 - 37 Punkte	36 - 23 Punkte	unter 23 Punkte
sehr gut bis gut	befriedigend bis ausreichend	nicht mehr ausreichend

___/46

Kapitel 4: Nomen

Aufgaben

1 **Seite 54**
a) guitar; it b) bike; it c) garden; it d) it
e) film; It f) car; it g) pencil case; it h) they
i) I; them j) book; it

2 **Seite 55**
a) **He** likes pasta.
b) **It** isn't our dog.
c) **Her** name was Sally. **She** was six.
d) **It** had a white cross on **its** back. My uncle's cat, Madonna, was lying on the carpet. When my sister started to scream because of the spider, **she** rushed after **it**.
e) Never trick an elephant. **It/He** will never forget.
f) Must **I** tidy up **her** cage today, Mum?
g) I can hear **him** barking in the garden.

3 **Seite 56**
a) a female elephant
b) two tomcats and a female dog
c) the princess and the duchess
d) the waitress saw the Prince of Wales
e) Peter's afraid of female spiders.
f) Were you in London last year? - Yes, I love her.

Seite 57 4
a) three men b) two pigs c) four bags d) five umbrellas
e) two cars f) six pianos g) ten trees h) three wardrobes
i) two gardens j) eleven windows k) three TV sets l) five friends

Seite 58 5
a) doors b) quays c) countries d) matches
e) lodges f) chimneys g) lorries h) batches
i) sprays j) witches

6
a) five calves b) six lorries c) a shelf d) ten kisses
e) three women f) two men g) a mouse h) all my teeth
i) three sheep j) two children

Seite 59 7
a) He showed courage when he climbed onto the roof of the house.
b) I like fish very much. Are these fish from the river?
c) His advice is always good.
d) Where did you get this information from?
e) She isn't blond, she's got black hair.

Seite 60 8
a) Where **are** my **trousers**? No idea, where can **they** be?
b) I must cut this sheet of paper. Do you know where the **scissors are**?
c) I can't find my **glasses**. Where are **they**?
d) I need **the scales** to weigh the letters. Where are **they**?
e) Look, there is a very beautiful bird in the garden. Go and get our **binoculars**. Can you find **them**?
f) I never wear **pyjamas** when I go to bed, but I wear **shorts**. I can't find **them**. **Are they** in the washing machine?

Seite 61 9
a) The thief stole the goods.
b) Wir verbrachten unsere Sommerferien in einer schönen Gegend.
c) wörtlich: Der Brief, den ich erhielt, war voller Dank. (Der Brief, den ich bekam, war ein Dankesbrief.)
d) Sie fiel die Treppe hinunter.
e) The shop is selling the new summer clothes.

Seite 63 10
a) four pairs of trousers (four jeans) b) three cups (and saucers)
c) two bottles of milk d) two slices of bread
e) five pieces of cake f) three pieces of advice
g) three kilos of sugar h) three pairs of glasses
i) two (pairs of) binoculars j) three pairs of shorts

Seite 64 11
A sad fellow: I don't have much money, but I've got many problems, few friends, some questions, little time, some patience and much trouble.
A happy fellow: I like many people, I've got few worries, much money, some friends, many hobbies and much patience.

Seite 65 12
a) Can I have **some** mustard, please. – I'm sorry, there isn't **any** left.
b) Did you hear that voice? Hello, is there **anybody**?
c) He has **some** good ideas, but he doesn't make **anything** out of them.
d) Pete didn't say **anything** interesting at the meeting.
e) What's the matter? Is **something** wrong? – Yes.
f) Fred needs **somebody/someone** to help him with his paper, but there isn't **anybody/anyone**.

g) Joe doesn't like **any** coffee. He likes tea.
h) Does **anybody/anyone** know where my mother is?

13 In my satchel I have got **a** pencil, **an** orange pen, **an** old book, **a** photo of my dog, **a** beautiful pencil case, **an** extra ruler and **a** used model car. Seite 66

14 a) a Norwegian fisherman b) Irish sheep c) dogs from England Seite 67
d) a Scottish bagpipe e) the roads in Wales f) My uncle's name is Tom.
g) I like Aunt Margaret. h) Our house is on King Street.
i) Can you see me, Dad?

Training plus

33 *it* (Singular), *they* (Plural) Seite 68

34 Länder, Städte und Fahrzeuge; außerdem vertraute weibliche Tiere, die mit Namen angesprochen werden

35 durch Anhängen von -s

36 Nomen auf Vokal endend, vorletzter Laut Vokal, z.B. *boy* → Plural: einfaches Anhängen von -s: *boys*; Nomen auf Vokal endend, vorletzter Laut ein Konsonant, z.B. *the cry* → Plural: Endung *-ies* statt *-y*: *the cries*

37 *pieces of information, bits of information*

38 *little* wird bei nicht zählbaren Nomen, *few* bei zählbaren Nomen verwendet: *little colour (wenig Farbe), few brushes (wenige Bürsten)*

39 *some:* in bejahten Aussagesätzen; *any:* in verneinten Aussagesätzen und Fragen

40 Nomen und Adjektive, welche Orte, Städte und Staaten bezeichnen oder sich auf diese beziehen.

Abschlusstest

1 a) **He** repaired **her** yesterday. But today **she** broke down again. I hope **we** will have **her** back soon. Seite 69
b) Did you see **him/her** in **it**? - No, I didn't, but I saw **her**. She was holding **it** in **them**.
c) **Her** shoes are not blue, **they**'re green and orange.
d) Great Britain is a nice place to spend a holiday. **She** is fantastic.
e) Why did the 'Titanic' sink? - **She** sank because she hit an iceberg. ___/14

2 I must buy three cans of cat fodder for my tomcat Tom, two pairs of scissors, a kilo of sugar, two knives, four cups, five bars of chocolate, two exercise-books for our neighbour's son, three wrist watches for my aunt's children, some ointment for my grandma's feet and three boxes of matches. ___/14

3 Last night I dreamt (dreamed) of three men and two women. They had big feet and few teeth. They talked to four children and played with six mice, two geese, four oxen and five sheep. Seite 70 ___/9

4 a) ~~informations~~, ~~They~~, ~~were~~
b) ~~Mathematic~~, ~~knowledges~~
c) ~~eye~~, ~~hairs~~
d) ~~luggages~~
___/5 e) ~~furnitures~~

5 I've got good news for you. You can spend your winter holiday in wonderful surroundings in
___/6 Austria. Take (some) pairs of trousers and a pair of binoculars with you.

Seite 71 6 a) **Some** people have a bike, but **few** people have a helicopter.
b) Have you got **some** time for me this weekend? - No, I haven't **any**.
c) Have you got 20 euros? - No, I've only got 1 euro. - Oh, that's **a little** money.
d) In Germany there are **many** people with no jobs at the moment. - Oh yes, that is really a big problem in **some** parts of the country.
e) Is there **anything** I must know? - No, there aren't **any** problems.
___/10 f) There is **something** to say about this man. He's mad.

7 a) **A** lion is a very dangerous animal from **A**frica. This animal lives in the central **A**frican plains. It's got **an** orange fur.
b) I bought **-** three watches in **a/the S**wiss shop.
c) I like **the G**erman football team very much. - No, I think **the E**nglish team is better. - But **the** best team is **the** team from **B**rasil.
d) I need **a** new pen, **an** orange pencil case, three **-** pens, my new T-shirt from **I**taly and my **S**panish book.
e) Listen, do you want to tell me **an** old story? I heard about this boy from **F**rance yesterday. My sister told me **the** story.
f) **B**avaria is a part of **G**ermany and **E**urope.
g) **An** apple **a** day keeps **the** doctor away.
___/36 h) **The** tiger is **an A**frican or **I**ndian animal.

___/90

90 – 72 Punkte	71 – 45 Punkte	unter 45 Punkte
sehr gut bis gut	befriedigend bis ausreichend	nicht mehr ausreichend

Anmerkung zu Aufgabe 2: Für jede Mengenangabe erhältst du einen Punkt, für die Mengenangaben mit richtigen Erweiterungen zwei Punkte.
Anmerkung zu Aufgabe 9: Für jede richtige Pluralform erhältst du einen Punkt.

Kapitel 5: Adjektive, Adverbien und adverbiale Bestimmungen

Aufgaben

Seite 72 1 **Many** people spend their holidays on campsites. They live in **big** caravans and are **happy** when the weather is **fine**. When the weather is **bad**, they often aren't so **happy**. Then you can see them walk around with **sad** faces and **small** umbrellas. But not all people are **sad**. Children often have **a lot of** fun in the rain. They try to hop across **muddy** puddles or are **excited** when they can walk through them. Their mothers do not think that this is **exciting**, because they have to wash the **dirty** clothes.

Seite 73 2 a) always b) never c) Sometimes d) always

3 Sandy sometimes writes letters. Sandy never reads books. Sandy always plays on the computer. Sandy often plays football. **Seite 74**

4 a) Every morning he has breakfast at a café in High Street. **Seite 75**
b) They are going to go to Britain tomorrow.
c) He leaves his house at 7.30 every day.
d) Every Sunday afternoon he rode his bike through the forest.
e) Sandra goes to her grandmother in Hatfield every weekend.
f) Last year he played the guitar at a club in Broad Street every Saturday.

5 a) He was born in London on the 11th of April in 1988.
b) I saw a film star at the station this morning.
c) She lost her dog in the underground last Tuesday in the morning.
d) Last week she went to the supermarket in Broad Street every afternoon.
e) She always bought a pound of butter there.

6 a) Last year he played the guitar in a club in Broad Street every Saturday. **Seite 76**
b) Every night his girlfriend was with him at a table next to the stage.
c) All evening he never looked at her from the stage.
d) On Sundays in the morning the young lady always reads the newspaper at breakfast in the dining room.
e) At the weekend I read the new Harry Potter on the sofa in my room all day long.
f) freie Schülerlösung

7 **Seite 77**

Adverb der Häufigkeit	Ortsangabe	Zeitangabe	Adjektiv
normally	**at school**	**in the morning before Christmas**	**funny**
always	**next to Sandra**	**after the holidays, at night**	**sweet**
never	**at my neighbour's house,**	**in summer**	**strong**
every Monday night	**in bed**	**every Monday**	**sad**
	at home		**nice**
			happy

Training plus

41 auf Nomen **Seite 78**

42 auf Verben, Adjektive, andere Adverbien und ganze Sätze

43 niemals zwischen Verb und Objekt; S **Adverb** P(V) ______ 0

44 *adverbs of frequency*

45 *always*

46 manchmal

47 *at 8.30*

48 *often*

49 nie, niemals

50 *at home*

51 am Abend, abends

52 für Nomen, die nicht Zählbares ausdrücken, z. B. *much time*

53 für Nomen, die Zählbares ausdrücken, z. B. *many trees*

54 Ort vor Zeit, Richtung vor Ort, Genaues vor Allgemeinem

Seite 79 **Abschlusstest**

___/3 1 Mr Miller never picks his nose at school in the morning.

2 Mike was in the cinema yesterday. He sat in row three. At first, he saw everything, but then a woman and a man took their seats in front of him. Mike said to the woman: "I never go to the cinema. Today I'm here and I want (would like) to see this film. Please look for new seats." The woman answered: "I'm sorry. My husband and I come here every Sunday at 6 o'clock in the evening. We always sit here." Then a fat man entered the cinema. He knew the woman. He said: "Hello, Margarete, you're here, too? I usually buy popcorn in the shop. But this evening I've got a free ticket and I forgot my money at home. Please pay for my popcorn tonight." ___/42

Seite 80 3
a) Sandra has her two piano lessons at school on Tuesdays and Fridays.
b) Sandra often practises the piano in the mornings. She sometimes practises the piano in the afternoons and in the evenings.
c) Sandra revises Maths on Mondays in the afternoon and on Wednesdays in the morning.
d) Sandra goes to the Movie Club on Thursdays in the evening.
e) Sandra plays football on Wednesdays in the afternoon.
f) Sandra's never got time for friends ___/12

Seite 81 4 Adjektive: angry, sad, lonely, happy, funny, nice; Adverbien der Häufigkeit: never, always, sometimes, every Wednesday; Adverbien der Zeit: in the morning, in the afternoon, at night, yesterday, in my holidays; Adverbien des Orts: at school, at the supermarket, in the city, in England; ___/19

5
a) Mike normally gets up at seven.
b) Sometimes he can sleep late in the morning.
c) Mike always goes to school by bike.
d) On Saturday in the morning his father never gives him a lift.
e) His father always says: "There's no bad weather, only the wrong clothes." ___/5

81 – 64 Punkte	63 – 40 Punkte	unter 40 Punkte
sehr gut bis gut	befriedigend bis ausreichend	nicht mehr ausreichend

___/81

Anmerkung zu Aufgabe 1: Für jedes richtige Satzglied gibt es 0,5 Punkte.
Anmerkung zu Aufgabe 2: Für jeden richtig übersetzten Haupt- oder Nebensatz (mit richtiger Zeitform, richtiger Personenendung usw.) gibt es 2 Punkte.

Kapitel 6: Präpositionen

Aufgaben

1 a) The lion is in front of the car. b) The dog is on the car. **Seite 82**
c) The giraffe is behind the car. d) The kangaroo is next to the tree.
e) The birds are in the trees. f) The trees are next to the car.
g) The boy is in the car.

2 a) Zwischen: The Johnsons' house is between the gym and the church. **Seite 83/84**
b) Gegenüber: There's an old tree opposite the fountain.
c) Unterhalb: Jenny's got a scar below her elbow.
d) Unter: There are five Englishmen among the pupils.
e) Auf dem Land: There's much fresh air in the country.
f) Hier, in der Schule: Susan isn't here, she's at school.
g) Unter: Where's my mobile phone? – It's under the chair.
h) In New York; auf der Straße: You can see many yellow taxis (cabs) in the streets in New York.
i) nach Boston; über Grönland hinweg: Today my father is flying to Boston. He's flying over Greenland (right now).

3 Ortspräpositionen: **Seite 85**

im	**in; at; on**	hinter	**behind**
vor	**in front of**	unter	**under; among**
zwischen	**between**	gegenüber	**opposite**
über (hinweg)	**above**	auf	**on**
unterhalb	**below**	darunter	**under**

4 a) The cat is **sleeping under** the chair.
b) Sarah is **waiting at** school. She's **sitting at a desk**.
c) Laura is **standing next to** Stan.
d) The dog is **barking behind** the bush.
e) Tim is **standing among** the students.

5 a) up b) down c) to d) away from **Seite 86**
e) into f) out of g) across h) past

6 a) … into the zoo … b) … out of the box … **Seite 87**
c) … past the lake … d) …past/round the tower …
e) … across the street … f) … through the garden …
g) … on the summit … h) … to the town hall …

i) … from the fence …
j) … up the stairs …
k) … … past me …
l) … down the ladder …

Seite 88

7 If you want to go **up** the hill, you go along the river. You walk **past** the big tree and go **across** the bridge. **Behind** the bridge there is a forest. At the end of the forest, there is a big rock. There are usually people standing **on** top of it. You walk **past** the rock and then you go **straight on** for some time and go **up** for a few minutes and reach a small pond. **Behind** the pond you can see the witch's cottage. You walk **past** the witch's cottage. **On** top of the hill there is a cross. Then you can see the lake **below** in the plain. Very often big birds fly **over** it.

Seite 90

8 a) In English speaking countries, children don't get their presents **on** Christmas Eve. They have to wait **until** Christmas Day.
b) **On** Christmas Eve people usually go to church **in** the evening.
c) **After** church, children hang a Christmas stocking close to the fireplace. **At** night Father Christmas comes **through** the chimney of the house and brings the presents. So **before** the children go to bed, they are usually very excited.
d) **In** the morning of Christmas Day, children usually get up very early to unwrap their presents. Many children already get up **before** six o'clock.
e) **In** the afternoon, Christmas dinner is served.
f) By the way: about hundred and sixty years **ago** people in Britain decorated the first Christmas trees.

Seite 91

9 a) I met her **at/in** school, **and** I asked her a lot of questions **because** she is very intelligent.
b) When I was **on** top of the hill, I had a wonderful view **of** the valley **and** I was absolutely happy.
c) **After** she had breakfast, she brushed her teeth **in** the bathroom.
d) Put the ruler **on** the table please, **and** then fix the new poster **onto/to** the wall.
e) I didn't find out what was happening, **because** Sue and Pete didn't tell me about it.

Training plus

Seite 92

55 Präpositionen der Zeit, der Richtung und des Ortes

56 *on the roof*

57 *under the exercise book*

58 *next to the door*

59 *behind you*

60 *in front of the tree*

61 *over/across the house*

62 *down*

63 *into*

64 *(away) from*

65 *upstairs*

66 *behind*

67 *In* ist statisch und bedeutet „im/in der", z.B. *in the castle*. *Into* ist eine Richtungspräposition und drückt Bewegung aus („in … hinein"), z.B. *into the theatre* (ins Theater hinein).

68 Konjunktion

69 vor (zeitlich): *before* oder *ago*; vor (räumlich): *in front of*

Abschlusstest

1 Mr Jorgesen is **at/in** a conference. Suddenly his boss looks **at** him. "Have you got your folder with you?" he asks. Mr Jorgensen looks everywhere: **in** his bag and **on** the desk. He can't find it. "I'm sure I put it **in** my bag this morning, but it's not there. It must be **at** home. I can call my wife **on** the telephone!" he says. He goes **to** the phone. The phone is **in front of** him **at** the window. "Hello! Oh, sweet baby, can I talk **to** Mummy, please?" Mr Jorgensen says **to** his daughter. His boss looks **at** him strangely. "Hello, darling, I forgot my folder. Can you please look **in/on** my desk. … Oh, it isn't there. Then it must be **on** the bedside table **in** our bedroom. … No? Then it can only be **under** the newspaper **on** the breakfast table. No? What? You threw the newspaper **in** the dustbin this morning? Bye, see you later **at** the party." **Seite 93** **___/20**

2 Mrs Miller is **in** the bank **in** Salisbury at the moment. Klaus is going **into** the bank. His money is **in** his pocket. Mrs Miller is putting all her money **into** her bag when Klaus sees a gangster coming **into** the building. He's got a gun **in** his hand! He waits for a moment **in** the building, then takes all the money, runs out and turns **into** Main Street. Thank God, the people **in** the bank are not **in** danger any longer. **___/11**

3 Präpositionen: in; up; in; into; to; until; on; out; to; in; in. **Seite 94**
Konjunktionen: and; after; because; and; and; while; But; and; and; because; and; and; and.

An einem Freitag Abend erlebten Andy und David ein lustiges Abenteuer im Garten. Nach dem Essen stellten sie ihr Zelt auf, weil sie darin schlafen wollten. Sie brachten ihre Schlafsäcke und ihre Taschenlampen ins Zelt und warteten auf die Nacht. „Wir könnten während der Nachrichten schlafen gehen", sagte Andy. „Nein, warten wir doch bis es dunkel ist," antwortete David. Es war jedoch Sommer und im Fernsehen kam ein guter Film und sie konnten nicht so schnell nach draußen gehen weil sie „Snakes and Ladders" mit Bianca und Tammy spielten. Als sie schließlich schlafen gehen wollten, regnete es in Strömen und Frau Smith sagte: „Ihr könnt heute Nacht nicht im Garten schlafen. Ihr werdet im Zelt nass werden!" **___/37,5**

4 Bonkers likes cars, so she is **in** the car very often. Sometimes, when it rains, she sleeps **under** the car, and when the sun shines, Bonkers likes to be **on** the car roof. After her nap she jumps **from** the car and stretches her legs **in front of** it. Then she usually walks **to** the other side of the car and wants to sleep again. But what's this? There are four dogs **in** the garden. They are **next to** the garden shed. Suddenly she is a cat alone **among** four dogs! She jumps **from/off** the car and runs **to** the tree. She climbs **up**. Now, she's a cat **on** the tree! But she can't go **down** again, because one of the four dogs is **between** the car and the tree. Bonkers is **in** a bad situation now. Can she get **out of** it? However, she's not **in** danger, because Mr Miller is coming **out of** his house to help her **out of** this terrible situation. **___/20**

Seite 95 5 It was about 150 years **ago**. A big sailing boat sailed **across** the Atlantic Ocean **to** South America. The sun was high **in** the sky and the wind was good. Suddenly the man **in** the mast shouted, "There is another sail there. I can see another ship!" The other sailors went **to** the side of the ship, but the other ship was still too far away. **In** the afternoon, right **after** lunch, the other ship was so close that they could read the name **on** its side **through** the telescope. It was Tinauticlus. But they couldn't see any people **on** the deck. "They must all be **in** their cabins!" the first mate said **to** the captain. **In** the evening, before he went **to/into** his cabin, the captain went **to** the first mate again. He was **at** the steering wheel. "I can't see a person **on** the deck. It's really spooky!" **In** the morning the ship was still **at** their side, so the captain thought, "Let's send some people." He and five sailors took a boat and rowed **to** the ship. They looked **in** every cabin, but the ship was empty! Nobody knows what happened. It is still a mystery. Some people think the Tinauticlus sailed **through/into** a storm, others say this ship was a ghost ship **on** its way **to** a dreamworld.

___/25

___/113,5

113,5 – 91 Punkte	90 – 56 Punkte	unter 56 Punkte
sehr gut bis gut	befriedigend bis ausreichend	nicht mehr ausreichend

Anmerkung zu Aufgabe 3: Für jede unterstrichene Konjunktion oder Präposition gibt es 0,5 Punkte.

Kapitel 7: Arbeitstechniken und Sprachfertigkeiten

Aufgaben

Seite 97 1 freie Schülerlösung

2

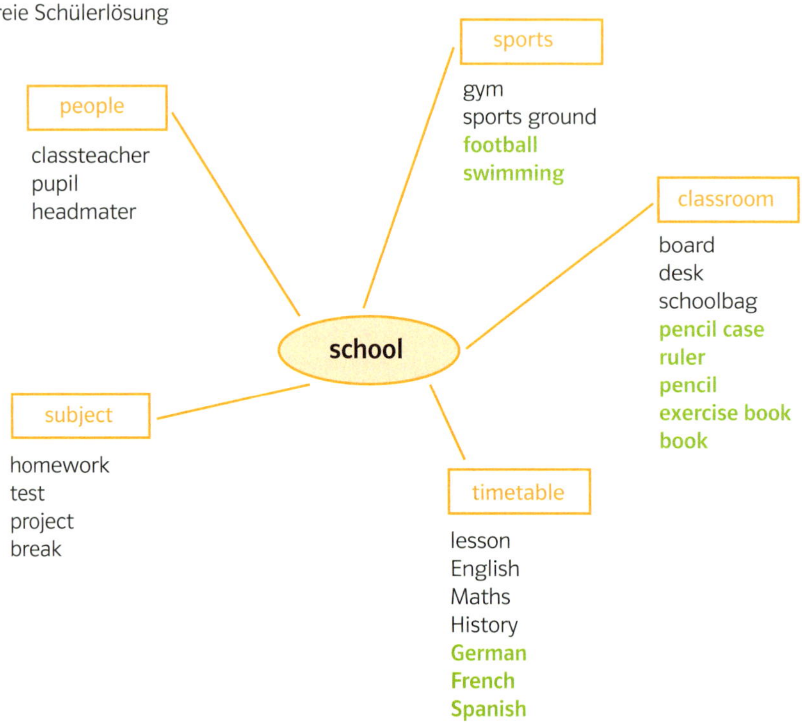

3 freie Schülerlösung **Seite 98**

4 freie Schülerlösung

5 freie Schülerlösung

6 Tipp: Lies dir den Text langsam vor. Gib nicht auf, wenn du einzelne Passagen auf Anhieb nicht so richtig verstehst. Versuche, die Gesamtzusammenhänge zu verstehen. **Seite 100**

7 **Seite 101/102**

a) false	b) false	c) false	d) false
e) false	f) false	g) true	h) true
i) true	j) true	k) false	l) false
m) true	n) true	o) false	p) true

8 **Seite 103**
a) The people in the story are Mike, Niki, her sister (the other girl) and the children's parents.
b) The story takes place on a beach in Greece.
c) The girls are from Germany.
d) They are sitting in the hotel restaurant.
e) The hotel is far away from the next town and there are no young people except the two girls.
f) His mother is shouting things across the beach.
g) The younger girl suddenly screams.
h) She's got a cut on her foot.
i) She speaks German.
j) They plan to go to the cinema.
k) Mike thinks that life can be so wonderful.
l) Yes, it does.

9 **Seite 104**
a) Hi, I'm Doris. I'm fourteen and I'm from Hamburg. Hamburg is a town in the north of Germany. My hobbies are swimming, reading books, chess and dancing.
b) May I introduce myself: I'm Mr Wagner. I'm very old. I'm from Augsburg. Augsburg is 60 kilometers northwest of Munich. My hobbies are playing the guitar, working with drama groups and writing English books.

10 **Seite 106**
a) I don't like cats, but I like dogs.
b) He prefers swimming to playing volleyball.
c) I hate computers, but I like reading newspapers.
d) He dislikes scooters, but he likes cars.
e) My favourite animals are monkeys.
f) Her favourite song is "Bleeding love".
g) Peter doesn't like football (American English: soccer).
h) Susan likes icecream. She likes doing the shopping.
i) My parents don't like snakes.

11 mögliche Lösungen: **Seite 107**

like/dislike

I like pop music but I also like rock music.
I like cats but I dislike dogs.
I like going to the cinema. I like going on holidays.
I dislike when you sing.

love
I love chocolate.
I love sunny days and I hate rainy days.

prefer
I prefer my coffee black.
I prefer cycling to walking.
I prefer stying at home.

hate
I hate being outside when it rains.
I hate doing the washing.

Training plus

Seite 108

70 z.B. Karteikasten, Mindmaps, Computerprogramme, Erstellen von Wortfeldern

71 Bedeutung, Schreibweise und Lautung

72 z.B.: *days* – *presents* – *family* usw.

73 z.B.: *Could you please repeat the sentence?*

74 *Who?*

75 *Where?*

76 *When?*

77 *What?*

78 *Why?*

79 *May I introduce myself, I'm … / Hello, I'm … / Hello, my name is …*

80 *How old are you?*

81 *dislike*

82 *hate*

83 *don't/doesn't like*

84 *favourite*

Abschlusstest

1 Seite 109

Verb	Adjektiv	Nomen
renew (erneuern)	**new (neu)**	**the news (die Neuigkeit; die Nachrichten)**
shock (schockieren)	shocking (schockierend)	**shock (der Schock)**
to slow (verlangsamen)	**slow (langsam)**	slowness (die Langsamkeit)
introduce (einführen)	introductory (Einführungs-)	**introduction (die Einführung)**
favour (bevorzugen; gerne mögen)	**favourite (Lieblings-)**	**favour (der Gefallen)**
understand (verstehen)	understandable (verstehbar; verständlich)	**understanding (Verstehen; Verständlichkeit)**
to make somebody happy (jemanden glücklich machen), to be happy (glücklich sein)	**happy (glücklich)**	happiness (das Glücklichsein)

__/13

2 z. B.: **in the air:** butterfly, bird, mosquito, bee etc.
on the ground: tiger, horse, pig, hamster, dog, cat, lion etc.
in the water: fish, crocodile, dolphin etc. __/7

3 Seite 110/111

a) Bavaria Wildlife Park has mammals, birds, reptiles, amphibians and insects.
b) The wildlife area is about 70000 acres (large).
c) You can have a meal at the Jungle Restaurant.
d) You can get information about wildlife and the threat to endangered animals.
e) It supports special projects.
f) In February the zoo closes at 4.30.
g) Three adults pay 24 €.
h) They must pay 36 €. __/16

4 Seite 111

a) May I introduce my sister to you?
b) I'm from Munich, a town in the south of Bavaria.
c) My hobby is reading books and I also like basketball.
d) Our favourite teacher is Thomas Cook.
e) Could you please repeat that sentence?
f) Could you speak more slowly, please?/Could you speak a bit slower, please?
g) Sorry, could you please spell that word?/Excuse me, could you spell that word, please?
h) I like English, but I dislike/don't like Maths. __/16

52 – 44 Punkte	43 – 26 Punkte	unter 26 Punkte
sehr gut bis gut	befriedigend bis ausreichend	nicht mehr ausreichend

__/52

Anmerkung zu Aufgabe 2: Für jede Vokabel erhältst du einen Punkt. Es gibt maximal 7 Punkte. Vorausgesetzt werden *dog, cat, hamster, horse, mouse, bird* und *fish*.

Seite 112/113

Training plus – zum Schluss

85 Das Grundmuster muss heißen: S-P-O.

86 Das *Present progressive* wird verwendet, wenn etwas gerade stattfindet.

87 Das *Simple present* wird verwendet, wenn etwas immer wieder geschieht, etwas immer so ist oder neue Handlungen einsetzen.

88 Als Hilfskonstruktionen dienen die Formen *doesn't* und *don't.*

89 *did, bought, slept*

90 *going to-future* (Anzeichen sind vorhanden) und *will-future* (etwas ist unausweichlich)

91 *much:* Verwendung bei Nomen, die nicht Zählbares ausdrücken.

many: Verwendung bei Nomen, die Zählbares ausdrücken.

92 Sie werden immer großgeschrieben.

93 Adjektive beziehen sich auf Nomen. Adverbien beziehen sich auf Verben, andere Adverbien oder ganze Sätze/Teilsätze.

94 *adverbs of place, adverbs of time, adverbs of direction*

95 **auf:** on
unter: under (räumlich), among (unter mehreren), below (unterhalb)
neben: next to
vor: in front of (räumlich), before (zeitlich vor einem Zeitpunkt), ago (Bezug auf Vergangenheit: vor 100 Jahren – hundred years ago)
hinter: behind

96 *ago*

97 Man benutzt den *of*-Genitiv.

98 Das ist zu mechanisch und führt kaum zum Lernerfolg.

99 Das klingt etwas barsch. Besser: *Would/Could you please repeat?*

Verbtabelle

Diese Liste wichtiger unregelmäßiger Verben enthält neben Infinitiv und *simple past*-Form auch die dritte Form, nämlich die des Perfekts (z.B. *to go - went - gone*; gehen - ging - gegangen). Diese dritte Form brauchst du zwar erst im sechsten Schuljahr, aber es ist äußerst vorteilhaft, das *perfect* gleich mitzulernen.

infinitive	simple past	perfect	deutsch
to be	was/were	been	sein
to beat	beat	beaten	schlagen, besiegen
to bring	brought	brought	bringen
to buy	bought	bought	kaufen
to choose	chose	chosen	wählen, aussuchen
to cling	clung	clung	festhalten, sich klammern
to come	came	come	kommen
to do	did	done	machen, tun
to draw	drew	drawn	zeichnen
to dream	dreamt	dreamt	träumen
to drink	drank	drunk	trinken
to drive	drove	driven	fahren
to eat	ate	eaten	essen
to fall	fell	fallen	fallen
to feed	fed	fed	füttern
to feel	felt	felt	(sich) fühlen
to fight	fought	fought	kämpfen, streiten
to find	found	found	finden
to fly	flew	flown	fliegen
to forget	forgot	forgot/forgotten	vergessen
to get	got	got/gotten	bekommen
to give	gave	given	geben
to go	went	gone	gehen
to grow	grew	grown	wachsen, anbauen
to have	had	had	haben
to hear	heard	heard	hören
to hit	hit	hit	treffen, schlagen
to hurt	hurt	hurt	weh tun, verletzen
to know	knew	known	kennen, wissen
to learn	learnt	learnt	lernen

infinitive	simple past	perfect	deutsch
to let	let	let	lassen
to lie	lay	lain	liegen
to lose	lost	lost	verlieren
to make	made	made	machen, tun
to mean	meant	meant	bedeuten
to meet	met	met	(sich) treffen
to put	put	put	setzen, stellen, legen
to read	read	read	lesen
to ride	rode	ridden	reiten, fahren
to run	ran	run	laufen, rennen
to say	said	said	sagen
to see	saw	seen	sehen
to send	sent	sent	schicken, senden
to set	set	set	setzen, stellen, legen
to shake	shook	shaken	schütteln
to shine	shined/shone	shined/shone	scheinen, glänzen
to shut	shut	shut	schließen, zumachen
to sing	sang	sung	singen
to sit	sat	sat	sitzen
to sleep	slept	slept	schlafen
to speak	spoke	spoken	sprechen
to spell	spelt	spelt	buchstabieren
to spend	spent	spent	verbringen, ausgeben
to stand	stood	stood	stehen
to swim	swam	swum	schwimmen
to take	took	taken	nehmen
to teach	taught	taught	lehren, unterrichten
to tell	told	told	sagen, erzählen
to think	thought	thought	denken, meinen
to throw	threw	thrown	werfen
to understand	understood	understood	verstehen
to wake	waked/woke	waked/woken	wecken
to wear	wore	worn	tragen
to win	won	won	siegen, gewinnen
to write	wrote	written	schreiben

Glossar

Abstrakte Nomen *(abstract nouns)*
Nomen oder Hauptwörter, die in dieser Form nur im → Singular verwendet werden können bzw. den → Plural mit Umschreibungen bilden müssen. Beispiel: *information, advice, water, homework.*

Adjektiv *(adjective)*
Gibt Auskunft darüber, wie etwas ist (Wiewort); steht vor → Nomen oder im Zusammenhang mit dem → Verb *to be*. Beispiel: *the nice boy; the boy is nice.*

Adverb *(adverb)*
Umstandswort. Gibt an, wie, wo, wie oft oder zu welcher Zeit man etwas tut. Beispiel: *happily, angrily; often, always, today, yesterday; here, there, ...*

Adverbiale Bestimmung
Umstandsbestimmung. Gibt an, wie, wo, wie oft oder zu welcher Zeit man etwas tut. Beispiel: *the right way, in angry tones, once a week, from time to time, under the car, behind the curtain, on Monday, in 1998 ...*

Aktiv *(active clause)*
Wenn das Subjekt des Satzes handelt, steht das Verb in der Aktiv-Form. Beispiel: *I read this book. - Ich lese dieses Buch*. Das Gegenteil ist das → Passiv.

Artikel, bestimmter *(definite article)*
Verweist auf eine näher bestimmte, bekannte Person oder Sache. Beispiel: *the green apple - der grüne Apfel.*

Artikel, unbestimmter *(indefinite article)*
Beschreibt eine nicht näher bestimmte Person oder Sache. Beispiel: *an apple; a green apple - ein Apfel; ein grüner Apfel.*

Demonstrativpronomen *(demonstrative pronoun)*
Wortart, mit deren Hilfe der Sprecher/die Sprecherin auf einen Gesprächsgegenstand verweist, auf den man z.B. mit dem Finger zeigen kann. Beispiel *this* (→ Singular), *these* (→ Plural); *that* (→ Singular), *those* (→ Plural).

Geschlecht, grammatisch *(gender)*
Ein Nomen kann männlich (Maskulinum), weiblich (Femininum) oder sächlich (Neutrum) sein. Das grammatische Geschlecht kann sich vom biologischen Geschlecht unterscheiden. Beispiel: *das Mädchen.*
Im Englischen spielt das Geschlecht bei der Satzbildung keine Rolle.

going to-future
Drückt aus, dass jemand etwas plant oder triftige Gründe oder Anzeichen dafür sprechen, dass etwas eintritt. Beispiel: *I <u>am going to</u> fly to Rio next week.*

Grundform *(infinitive)*
Infinitiv des → Verbs ohne Hinweise auf Personen oder Zeitform (Tempus). Beispiel: *drive, eat, drink ...*

Häufigkeitsadverb *(adverb of frequency)*
Gibt an, ob eine Handlung oft, manchmal, immer, regelmäßig, normalerweise, selten oder nie stattfindet. Beispiel: *often, sometimes, always, regularly, normally, rarely, never ...*

Hilfsverb, modales *(modal auxiliary verb)*
Kann nur in Verbindung mit einem → Vollverb das → Prädikat eines Satzes bilden. Beispiel: *I <u>must</u> help my father this afternoon. Jenny <u>can</u> play football!*

Imperativ *(imperative)*
Befehlsform des Verbs. Beispiel: *Help me! Shut up, please.*

Infinitiv *(infinitive)*
→ Grundform des → Verbs.

Konsonant *(consonant)*
Mitlaut. Beispiel: *[p, t, k]* Das Gegenteil ist der → Vokal (Selbstlaut).

Mengenanzeiger *(quantifiers)*
Bezeichnen bestimmte oder unbestimmte Mengen und stehen in der Regel vor den zählbaren oder nicht zählbaren → Nomen. Beispiel: *some juice, any bottles, much money, little work, every pupil, all teachers, a lot of time.*

Modales Hilfsverb *(modal auxiliary verb)*
→ Hilfsverb

Nomen *(noun)*
Substantiv oder Hauptwort; wird oft von einem → Artikel begleitet. Beispiel: *flower, stone* …

Objekt *(object)*
Satzergänzung; Satzglied im 3. Fall (Dativobjekt; Frage: Wem?) oder 4. Fall (Akkusativobjekt; Frage: Wen oder Was?)

Ortsadverb und adverbiale Bestimmung
Zum Beispiel *here, there, at school, in the park, under the car* …

Paarwort *(pair noun)*
Bezeichnet Dinge, die aus zwei Teilen bestehen und im → Plural gezählt werden. Beispiel: *scissors, trousers, jeans, glasses*…

Passiv *(passive clause)*
Das Subjekt eines Satzes handelt nicht selbst, sondern etwas wird mit ihm gemacht bzw. es „erleidet" eine Handlung. Das Verb steht dann in der Passiv-Form. Beispiel: The car was stolen. – Das Auto wurde gestohlen. Das Gegenteil ist das → Aktiv.

Personalpronomen *(personal pronoun)*
Steht anstelle eines → Nomens. Beispiel (Subjektfall):
I, you, he, she, it, we, you, they.

Plural *(plural)*
Mehrzahl. Beispiel: *flowers, stones* …. Das Gegenteil ist der → Singular.

Possessivpronomen *(possessive pronoun)*
Besitzanzeigendes Fürwort; zeigt an, wem etwas gehört oder wem etwas zuzuordnen ist. Beispiel: *my, your, his, her, its, our, your, their.*

Prädikat *(predicate)*
Satzaussage; besteht aus einem → Vollverb oder aus einem Verb und einem Hilfsverb. Beispiel: *He likes pizza. She must play the trumpet.*

Präposition *(preposition)*
Verhältniswort; drückt im Satz das Verhältnis von Personen und Dingen zueinander aus. Es gibt z.B. → Präpositionen des Ortes, der Richtung oder der Zeit.

Präposition des Ortes *(preposition of place)*
Beschreibt den Ort von Dingen und Personen. Beispiel: *on, under, next to, in front of, behind* …

Präposition der Richtung *(preposition of direction)*
Verrät etwas über eine Richtung oder Bewegung. Beispiel: *up, down, to, into, around, through*

Pronomen *(pronouns)*
Wörter, die für (lateinisch: pro) ein Nomen stehen. Durch sie vermeidet man z.B die Wiederholung eines Nomens. Es gibt z.B. → Personalpronomen oder → Possessivpronomen.

Present progressive (Verlaufsform der Gegenwart)
Drückt aus, was im Moment des Sprechens passiert bzw. was jemand im Moment des Sprechens tut. Beispiel: ***It is raining at the moment. Susi and Pete are playing football.*** Signalwörter für das *present progressive* sind zum Beispiel ***at the moment, now.***

Richtungspräposition *(preposition of direction)*
→ Präposition der Richtung

Satz *(sentence, clause)*
Ein vollständiger Aussagesatz besteht mindestens aus einem Subjekt und einem Prädikat. Die Satzstellung *(word order)* im englischen Aussagesatz folgt dem Muster Subjekt - Verb/Prädikat - Objekt bzw. ***subject - verb/predicate - object (S - P - O).***

Satzglied
Teil des Satzes. Besteht aus einem Wort oder einer Wortgruppe. Beispiel: ***My dog/hates/ black cats.*** Die bekanntesten Satzglieder sind Subjekt ***(subject)***, Prädikat ***(predicate)*** und Objekt ***(object)***.

Simple past
Einfache Vergangenheit; gibt in der Vergangenheit abgeschlossene Handlungen wider. Beispiel: I ***watched TV last night***. Signalwörter für das *simple past* sind zum Beispiel: ***last week, yesterday, three years ago.***

Simple present (einfache Gegenwartsform)
Wird verwendet, wenn etwas immer wieder so passiert oder immer wieder so ist. Beispiel: ***We always <u>have</u> breakfast in the kitchen. Every morning, he <u>gets up</u> late.*** Signalwörter für das *simple present* sind zum Beispiel ***always, every, usually.***

Singular *(singular)*
Einzahl. Beispiel: ***flower, stone … Das Gegenteil ist der → Plural.***

Subjekt *(subject)*
Satzgegenstand; Satzglied im 1. Fall bzw. Nominativ; Frage: Wer?/Was?). Beispiel: ***The teacher sounds angry.***

Unzählbare Nomen *(noncounts/noncountables)*
Beispiele: ***love, milk, information***

Verb *(verb)*
Tätigkeitswort oder Zeitwort. Beispiel: ***walk, he talked, he has lost.***

Verb, unregelmäßig *(verb, irregular)*
Bildet die Vergangenheitsformen unregelmäßig. Beispiel: ***drive - drove - driven; go - went - gone***.

Vokal *(vowel)*
Selbstlaut. Beispiel: *[a, o, u]*. Das Gegenteil ist der → Konsonant (Mitlaut).

Vollverb *(main verb)*
Kann allein das → Prädikat eines Satzes bilden, d.h. ohne ein → Hilfsverb. Beispiel: ***Elephants eat a lot!***

Will-future
Drückt Vorhersagen oder Vermutungen über die Zukunft aus, die nicht beeinflussbar sind oder verweist auf spontane Entschlüsse. Beispiel: ***It will be cloudy tomorrow. Wait, I will help you!***

Zeitadverb bzw. -adverbial
yesterday, last week, today, in 1988, on Mondays …

Zeit/Zeitform *(tenses)*

Zeit lässt sich in die Bereiche Vergangenheit, Gegenwart und Zukunft aufteilen. Zeit wird durch die Zeitformen *(tenses)* ausgedrückt. Beispiel: ***present tense: simple present*** und ***present progressive; past tense: simple past*** und ***past perfect; future: will-future*** und ***going to-future.***

Zeitpräposition *(preposition of time)*

Gibt an, wann oder zu welchem Zeitpunkt etwas passiert. Beispiel: ***10 years ago, before, on, in, at, during …***

Zischlaut

Laut, der mit einem hörbaren Pfeifen oder Zischen einhergeht. Beispiel: ***to watch, to kiss.***

Stichwortverzeichnis